More Praise for
Tears Are the Source of Your Passion

In today's times of seeing and feeling so much pain, bewilderment, and grief in our world, these personal stories and heart-deepening lessons by Chris & Mandy are urgent teachings for authentically approaching, intentionally mining, and learning to truly celebrate our universal human experiences of heartbreak, defeat and loss. This book is not just for those in a period of intense grief but, is for EVERYONE and ANYONE who genuinely wants to keep an open heart and an awakened mind toward the richness of living life to the fullest!

~Tammy Anderson Starling, LPC-MHSP, Psychotherapist and Grief Specialist

An empowering guide for every healing journey, "*Tears*" offers rare heart-opening wisdom into the transformative power of grief that every human being deserves to know. This life-affirming book ignites hope and nurtures the soul!

~Elizabeth Catignani, author of *Creative Grieving*: A Hip Chick's Path from Loss to Hope

This book celebrates the fullness of our humanity. It confronts the widely held, destructive belief that leads us to feel ashamed of our grief and struggles. Saade and Bird present a brilliant model that guides us to navigate our experiences of personal and global heartbreak in ways that bring strength, pride, and dignity. I am very excited about applying these ideas in my work with young people.

~Barry Sherman, MSW, LCSW, School Social Worker/SEL Coordinator

Being a gerontologist, I've read many books on grief and loss. This book has a depth of heart and soul that could not have been manifested at a better time for the whole of humanity. The process in this unique model is not linear or "prescribed" but one that is personalized to each griever's unique style when reacting to profound loss. The approach brings those in grief to a place of seeing gifts in even the most devastating losses.

~Lyndall Hare, Ph.D, Gerontologist

This book is a life-giving resource for re-discovering your way to passion and meaning through your grief experiences. Using a broad psychological and spiritual approach, these pages explore the meaning of grief and help reorient your perspective toward the grief that strikes each of our lives sooner or later! The perfect gift for a loved one who is grieving or your own grieving heart to discover that choosing to mine your grief can crack open your heart and guide you toward your most authentic and meaningful life.

~Ginger Wagoner, Photographic Artist and pursuer of justice

ALSO BY CHRIS SAADE

Second Wave Spirituality:
Passion for Peace, Passion for Justice

Prayers for Peace and Justice

Prayers from the Heart
Love, Sacred Activism, and Praise

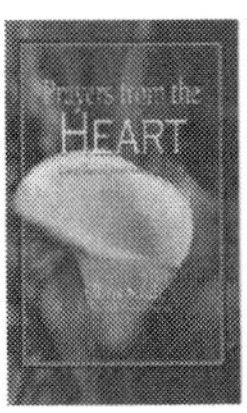

Prayers from the Heart is also available in audio format with narration by Andrew Harvey at **www.audible.com**

Evolutionary Love Relationships:
Passion, Authenticity, and Activism

An Evolutionary Vision of Relationships:
the Spirituality of Romantic Love

Sacred Activism & the
Epic Spirituality of Love

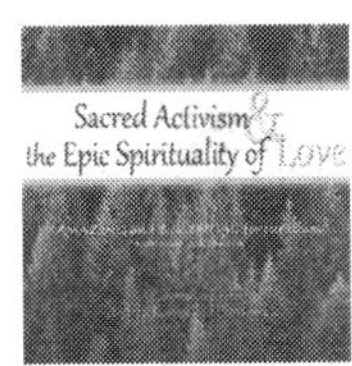

Rebellion of the Heart:
Deep Authenticity, Bold Love, Passion, Strength, and Global Solidarity

Chris Saade & Mandy McMullen Bird, M.A., LCMHC

Roundtable Productions
San Diego, CA

FIRST EDITION
Published by ROUNDTABLE PRODUCTIONS, 2303 Darlington Row, La Jolla, CA 92037
Chris Saade's publications are available through most bookstores. For further information, visit:
www.facebook.com/ChrisSaadeAuthor/

ROUNDTABLE PRODUCTIONS
San Diego, CA

Cover design and illustration: Stephanie Dalton Cowan / daltoncowan.com / daltonprojects.com
Mandy McMullen Bird photo by Tess Brico
Original compilation of interviews by Janet Thomas
Edited by: Ginger Wagoner and Casey Robertson
General support: Ginger Wagoner
Publisher logo by sam_designz on fiverr.com
Library of Congress Cataloging-in-Publication Data is available on request.
Saade, Chris, 1950-, co-author; Bird, Mandy McMullen, 1966-, co-author
Tears Are the Source of Your Passion / Chris Saade and Mandy McMullen Bird
Issued in print and electronic formats.
ISBN 978-0-9903140-5-9

To everyone whose heart has been broken and/or body deeply wounded—my profound respect and empathy.

~**Chris Saade**

This book is lovingly dedicated to my Grandmothers, Virginia Amanda Kinsell McMullen and Shirley Ethel Warner Hayes. Your love helped to fuel my passion & soothed my heartbreak.
You are always with me.
And to my heart cherished KP, gone too soon. Life is never the same without you.
I will miss you until my final day!

~**Mandy McMullen Bird**

Let Me Tell You About Mandy Bird

I am very honored and blessed to have co-written this book with my dearest friend, Mandy Bird.

Let me tell you a bit about Mandy. Mandy has been, and continues to be, an incredible advocate for the heart, authenticity, and for the grief we inescapably carry as human beings. Not only is she exceptionally skilled at counseling people in freeing their heart, affirming their unique authenticity, and honoring their grief; she also offers her support with a stunning level of care, compassion, and commitment to those with whom she works.

Mandy has spent most of her life listening to the wounds of individuals and bringing dignity to their tears. She has sat with the suffering and the broken-hearted and helped them transform their relationship with their pain and mine vision and passion from their wounds.

Mandy has co-written this book from the depth of her soul. She has poured her knowledge into it as well as colored it with her own intimate knowing of vulnerability and pain. She has brought to it her own sense of undying hope. I have been very enriched writing this book with her. The journey of manifesting *Tears Are the Source of Your Passion* has been a balm to my own wounds and a step further into allowing the river of creative and compassionate passion flow through my own heart.

There are so many more honorings one can offer about Mandy, however I believe this book will reveal a great deal about her most helpful, generous, and wise spirit.

~Chris Saade

TABLE OF CONTENTS

SECTION ONE

SECTION TWO

7 Steps Toward the Power of Grief and Hope℠

Acknowledgements from Chris Saade

This book represents the edge of my work around the sacred relationship between grief and passion. Therefore, it is fitting to express my deeply felt gratitude to those going through a great grief who are willing to and *choose to* invest in this exploration of the inseparable connection between grief and passion—two pillars of the life force. I honor you who feel your heart deeply, who care intensely for the freedom of your authenticity, and who stand for the great dream of solidarity. At a time in our world when most religious and spiritual dogmas compete in rigidity, when indifference, denial, and cynicism have become a trend, and when hate and divisiveness are erected as political choices, I am awed by how much we owe to the people of heart. Such brave individuals are my inspiration and, I believe, the impetus for a viable future. That you would invest yourself in love and service during a time of darkness and pain, contributes to hope in the world and makes you truly heroic. Thank you from the depths of my heart, and on behalf of humanity and our Earth.

I also want to express profound gratitude for all those closest to my heart for your support, love, insights, feedback challenges, and partnership.

To Mandy Bird, my dearest friend, co-author, and faithful advocate of grieving hearts, I am so grateful for all the heart, mind, and soul you have invested in this book. You have done so with beautiful passion and generosity. You are a gift and a blessing to me, your family, your friends, and all of our community.

To my precious daughter, Amal Maria, I cannot thank you enough for our rich conversations, your loving support, and beautiful theatrical artistry and community work that supports children and promotes authenticity and solidarity through drama. You endlessly inspire me. I am also very grateful for my highly caring and gifted actor son-in-law, Vince. And, of course, you and my daughter have given me the unspeakable joy of becoming a grandfather to two incredible and adorable spirits!

To Casey Robertson, my soul sister, I celebrate the depth of work that you continually do on a daily basis—diving to depths like a whale to live your life authentically and generously. Your pursuit of authenticity creates such rich wisdom for our dialogues which are wonderful fodder for my writing and teaching.

To Barry Sherman, my soul brother, you have my incessant gratitude for our cherished friendship and your commitment to serve children and champion the underprivileged. You are unfailingly with me when I write.

To Jessie Thompson, I am so grateful for your multi-level support for the creation of this book. Your soulful investment in this book has been very generous and meant a lot to Mandy and me.

To my soul-sister and editor, Ginger Wagoner, I offer great gratitude. As you always do, you have poured yourself generously into this book with insightful edits, clarifications, and suggestions. Your heart-commitment and skills are invaluable!

To my journey companions of Authenticity and Solidarity not mentioned elsewhere—Tammy Starling, Cindy Ballaro, Lyndall Hare, Holly Britt Warren, and Lawrence Petersen—you have my love and enduring gratitude for all we have shared, and all we strive for in this world.

I also extend my gratitude to my dearest journey heart-companions and friends. I feel deeply connected with your spirit and words through the learning circles of the Institute for Life-Leadership and Coaching (theilc.org). I am indebted to you for participating in our countless weekend retreats of deep hearted exploration, practicing cutting-edge relationship tools, and supporting one another's raw authenticity and desire for social solidarity. Your intelligence, humor, dedication to authenticity, and pursuit of love-in-action have contributed greatly to the revelations contained in this book. And now with Tom Anthony as the director of the ILC, you are bringing so much heart and wisdom to fortunate students!

Acknowledgements from Mandy Bird

There are so many amazing people to thank for their support, friendship, and love. And so many who have inspired me and brought rich meaning and beauty to my life. Here is the short list of some of my biggest supporters and those for whom I am forever grateful!

To my dear beloved soulmate and husband Glenn, we waited a long time to find each other and finally did—in this lifetime—thru grace. My gratitude for you is only surpassed by the depth of my love and respect for you. Thank you for being by my side and supporting me through the long road of this project. Your belief in me and what is possible through me means the world to me and is a bright light when things look dim. I so fully appreciate your love and caring for me in the details that allowed me to go for this book and for other passions! I love you through all time and eternity! I am forever grateful and aware of how fitting it is that the Angel of Grief was the spark that brought us together. Thank you for walking hand in hand thru this beautiful and heartbreaking life with me, my beloved G. Bird.

To my life's great true love, my beloved daughter Tess Amanda, Oh how you shine... oh how your spirit teaches me every day. I am so happy to be molded and sculpted and taught by your authentic being. You show me things about myself to which I've been blind. I am blessed beyond measure to have a thoughtful, brilliant, beautiful, deeply-caring-for-justice daughter such as you! My heart surrounds you always with my ferocious love! May you always remember that when life cuts you, it will also bring you beauty, for paradox always exists my precious darling. Always hold the beauty of the world in your heart! I love you!!!!

Thinking back to the first time I met my coauthor, Chris Saade, in Spring of 1997, I feel incredibly grateful for the many years of fierce mentoring support, incredible wisdom and continually uplifting belief in my leadership gifts and abilities. Chris, you have offered me a dear brotherly friendship bar none! Thank you for inviting me to join you in this vital book project! I am so honored and deeply blessed to have shared in this process with you! May our words reach every single human being that needs them!!! I love you dearly!!!

I would not have been able to make this book a reality without the brilliant detail holding and consistent practical and soulful support of my dear soul-sister and friend Ginger Wagoner. Truly, your ability to hold the details, continue to brainstorm for another idea and another idea for our book to breakthrough, and the love you demonstrated to me through the years of manifesting this much needed book has been astounding! I am forever grateful that you agreed to be my right-hand woman! Oh how lovely, smart, and talented you are! How blessed I've been by the level of excellence you bring! You are a one-in-a-million diamond of a goddess!

My deep and devoted soul friendship with the one and only Tammy Starling has been an unending source of inspiration in watching and learning how you have danced your grief since December 8, 1989. You have taught me much with beauty and grace, and have matched my determination and tenacity unlike any other! I am grateful always for your love, our shared joys, and shared laughter!! You truly are one stellar human being... a radiant star! Your faith, wisdom, support, and loyalty have been a rock in my life! Oh the places we have been and the things we've seen... lots of heartbreak and immense beauty! What a blessed woman of God you are!!!

To Casey Baxter Robertson... a muse unlike any other that walks this earth! Our bond and hunger in seeking authentic freedom while honoring the authentic truth of our wounds has carved a permanent place in my heart! I would not be as free as I am in my bold seeking and pursuits if it were not for your love and example!

To Barry Sherman... a brother of my heart! Thank you for your dogged friendship and tireless pursuit of mining your own gifts and giving them so generously to the world! I am mentored by your generous life and sharp mind. To see you use your many artistic and scholarly talents to serve is like watching fine art in motion. You are a gift to so many!

It is so important to me to thank my parents Pat and Shirley McFadden, and Mike and Leslie McMullen. In my adult life, I have truly been lifted up and have felt your parental support and pride. There are so many things to be thankful for. Thank you Pat for teaching me about fierce loyalty. Thank You Mom for teaching me about vital nurturing support. Thank you Dad for teaching me about undying love. Thank you Leslie Carol for teaching me about endless faith. I am so grateful to be loved and to call each of you my parents. God knew what S/he was doing in assigning my spirit four parents.

Thank you to my additional three dear soul-sisters. Here are just a few of the qualities you possess which have helped bolster my spirit through the years. Holly Britt Warren, for your no-holding-back around both grieving big and loving big! Cindy Ballaro, for your effervescent joy, your contagious belief in what is possible, and for always being in my corner! Lyndall Hare, for your unfaltering passion, brilliant creativity, and caring so fully for the world's aging.

Thank you with all my heart to my dear Aunt Maxine and my precious cousin Kenda Lou. Each of your love for me and support throughout my life has lifted me up when I needed it! Your big faith and our shared love of the Divine has been a deep source of comfort for me!

My dear brother and sister-in-law, Jess Michael and Tina Bone.... For many foodie nights during the years that my heart was broken open. Those family times meant more to me than I can ever express.

Monica Joye... for all the years upon years of laughter, confidences, tears, and dreams. Thank you for always sitting with me in my grief and my joy! I love you immensely... always!!!

Foreword

My friends, we are living in an age when the whole of humanity's heart is being broken because of what is happening *in* our world and *to* our world. The journey of grief can be the story of our demise, OR we can make it our story of the "alchemy of agony"—the transmutation of our suffering into resplendent gifts to others and to our world itself.

This book revisits ancient wisdom in profoundly new and concrete ways. Rumi expressed it exquisitely:

Suffering is a treasure, for it conceals mercies;
The almond becomes flesh when you peel off the rind.
O my brother, staying in a cold place
And bearing patiently grief, weakness, and pain,
Is the Source of Life and the cup of Abandon!
The heights are found only in the depths of abasement;
Spring is hidden in autumn, and autumn pregnant with spring.
Flee neither: be the friend of Grief ...

What is being offered within these pages is precisely what Rumi knew to be possible... a guide to reach the gold through your grief... a path forward when you are suffering, aching with pain that seems as though it is devouring you, and feeling stuck or even drowning in grief. First, if you are considering taking your own life, get professional support *immediately*. Second, do your best to find professional support that excels in grief work that does NOT encourage you to bury your grief. Third, bless your self and your grief with the wisdom contained in this book. It will nurture you, give you hope, and help you uncover precious treasures that await you in your grief.

Seldom, in all my years of pursuing and championing sacred activism, do I encounter teams as dynamic, dedicated, and as willing to dive deep into excavating the heartbreak of the world as the team of Chris Saade and Mandy Bird! This "dynamic-duo" first opened their hearts to me years ago, and as they have become precious friends and partaken in what I have to share, they have also illuminated my mind in incredible and nuanced understandings around our shared passion for grief and its hidden blessings.

Over the years, Chris has shared extreme and poignant personal stories with me around his own grief, some of which he shares in this book. Chris was a victim of abuse in his childhood. He then lived through the war in Lebanon and became a leader in the peace movement there. He has seen and experienced horrors many of us cannot begin to fathom. He has a gentle soul, and is a brother to all grievers. He has dedicated his life to empowering individuals in their authenticity through his personal coaching, lecturing, workshops, and multiple books. I trust him with my life and with my grief.

Likewise, Mandy has endured many grief-experiences that would lead many to end their own lives. But, like Chris, she has allowed her traumas to lead her to counsel others along the grief journey and to help them mine the treasures buried within their own grief. For a time, Mandy was the director of The Respite, a grief center she co-founded. Through this non-profit, she dedicated herself to helping others experiencing great personal losses reach into their tragedies and emerge having discovered the ways they are called to serve the world. Similarly, Mandy is one of very few people I would turn to in a time of grief. She is a soul-sister and an angel of mercy for many in deep pain.

Together in this book, Chris and Mandy have assembled their collective wisdom around the grieving process (and it *is* a process). The duo approaches grief philosophically, spiritually (in a manner inclusive of all beliefs), and with concrete tools and activities for the griever to use in their own time to help along the grief journey. Demonstrating full respect for the grieving process and the time it takes, they explain the essential nature of the passion-grief relationship. They reveal the path to empowerment that is born out of this relationship. The blessing of paradoxical feelings and experiences is examined. And, most importantly, the interrelationship of our authenticity and serving the global grief of the world is revealed.

My passion for this book and the work Chris and Mandy are offering the world is profound! So many are paralyzed by grief, and there are times in my life when I, myself, have felt paralyzed by grief. There is no shame in that. But now is the time to wake up. This book is the guide to helping us awaken. Your grief has the power to birth you into sacred activism as mine has birthed me.

This book is crucial because it offers an approach to personal grief work that splits the atom of the false self and allows it to explode into authentic service for justice and compassion. It uses heartbreak in a radical way—breaking new territory, it escorts us through the essential energy of grief and helps us process it in a vibrant way by helping each individual discover their own unique way into service for humanity and Mother Earth.

What begins as grief, transmutes into global blessings. What better alchemy could there be?! There is no book more relevant to today's crises.

~Andrew Harvey, Internationally acclaimed poet, novelist,translator, mystical scholar, spiritual teacher, and author of over 30 books.
2021

Introduction

There is nothing more important than living an authentic, meaningful, and passionate life. It is essential for each individual and crucial for our world today. When we bravely choose to feel and engage our grief consciously and with wisdom, our heart can blossom with love and a meaningful vision—we come to know the fullness and passion of life and the sacred power which life has in store for us. Grief is an unavoidable part of our life-journey. There are losses so big that the heart shatters, and it seems as if our world is collapsing. Yet we can learn to powerfully and creatively transmute these losses into a fertile ground where more love can grow. The tears of our deepest grief can become a wellspring of great passion. The brokenness that gives us so much sorrow can also become the channel through which greater love can flow—but only if we powerfully choose to keep our heart open and refuse to shut down in bitterness and paralyzing despair.

Grief is one of the sacred doors into our passion. It is extremely rare to find people living their passion who have not experienced significant loss and suffering. We can learn to use our grief as a powerful force to help us clear away the fog of superficiality and find the deeper waters of what matters most in our life. It can become a great definer and great clarifier. Paradoxically, as painful as grief is, there is the possibility for us to focus and forge our grief into a spark that ignites our passion. Empowered individuals throughout time have mastered the art of extracting greater strength, self-knowing, and capacity to love from the wounds and heartbreak they have endured. This sacred skill has largely been buried under misguided belief systems that keep us either victimized by our grief or in denial of it. Encountering our grief from a place of centered power can help us discover more of our deepest authenticity and the calling of our heart.

Our capacity to feel grief is as much part of our humanity as our ability to feel joy. These two rivers of feeling, grief and joy, are the life-blood of who we are as human beings. We have evolved over millions of years to have feelings, and each feeling is essential and enables us to experience and come to know the world, each other, and our own authenticity. Our feelings are powerful bonds that connect us to each other and to the Earth. Grief and joy are life-giving forces: grief is a force that spurs us to create and evolve and provides powerful fuel for standing up to the forces of oppression, and joy is a force that nourishes our body and soul and gives us the strength to choose hope.

However, courageous acts of grieving, feeling joy, and holding hope are also critical *skills* that we must consciously master in order to engage our passion. As human beings we are being called to understand that grief, joy, and hope are not just feelings which visit us, they are essential wisdoms and responsibilities we are asked to develop. *Tears Are the Source of Your Passion* provides some of the tools and wisdom that will help you become a skilled griever and courageous holder of joy and hope. These powerful steps will guide you in using these skills to claim greater authentic freedom and to powerfully serve love and justice in our struggling world.

The destructive ideologies of positive thinking and superficial transcendence, or alternately, the extremes of nihilistic cynicism, sarcasm, and apathy have greatly hindered our ability to powerfully and creatively engage with our grief. Grief must be differentiated from untethered emotionality, extreme negative thinking, and depression; and hope must not be confused with superficial denial or blind naivety. Our ability to feel all our deep and genuine feelings—whether happiness, excitement, peace, sadness, anxiety, or outrage—is crucial to the development of our mind and the expansion of our intelligence. But regrettably, throughout the history of human empires, there have been ideologies that have oppressed and continue to repress the human heart and our ability to feel deeply and genuinely. Our grief, which we have been taught to repress and avoid the most, is actually a tremendous source for our soul-making, both as individuals and as a nation. Collectively, we have forgotten that our capacity to feel is a wellspring of great power, wisdom, and creativity. Culturally we lack the support, knowledge, and tools that enable us to encounter and channel powerful feelings such as grief toward greater authenticity, freedom, justice, and love—in other words to claim the fullness of our humanity with grace and dignity! Becoming a mature and skilled griever enriches our lives in extraordinary ways that bless our loved ones and our communities.

Our grief—be it in the form of sadness, anger, or anxiety—is our natural, creative, and life-giving response to the great difficulties of our human condition as well as to the forces of oppression which threaten us. Sadly, our grief has taken the brunt of cultural as well as spiritual repression. We have been taught to hide, disparage, and be ashamed of the grief we feel around our wounds, losses, and defeats as we move through our life. This has led to an epidemic of isolation, denial, despair, and addiction as we are unable to be real and transparent with each other and with our own self. There is no shame in grief. In fact, grief, when ennobled and experienced mindfully, becomes the great creative force that leads us to love more deeply and, when needed, to stand strongly against oppression. To deny and shame our grief is to cut ourselves off from the vital life force of our own authenticity. We must learn to stop avoiding and numbing our grief and, instead, get to know it in its true reality, feel it, and learn how to mine it for wisdom about our own being, the world, and our passion. We are asked to awaken to a dawn of profound authenticity and a daring social, economic, and ecological solidarity. Without claiming our grief and understanding how to honor our defeats, we live a barricaded life—shutting ourselves away from greater love and greater intelligence.

This book is an invitation to root yourself deeply in loving and respecting your full story—the beauty and victories of your life as well as the losses and defeats—to welcome them all as sacred parts of your glorious humanity. You will *not* find recommendations for how to shorten or avoid any part of what it means to be fully human. However, you *will* find support for the grand heroic journey of your own heart. This book is for those who are hungry to mine the treasure from their grief and to discover the beautiful truth that our pain does not need to be in vain.

We need to discover and understand how our grief can enrich our life and expand our sense of calling. Learning to honor our grief leads us to accept that life itself is wounded, a paradox of beauty and

> It is critical to understand that genuine feelings and rational thinking do not contradict each other. To the contrary, they actually go hand in hand. People often confuse unexamined thoughts for feelings, however, muddy and confused thoughts are neither true feelings nor good thinking. A feeling is a profound emotion that arises from the heart and then unfolds through clear and rational thinking. Setting the heart and mind in opposition can lead to a chaotic sentimentality on the one hand and repression of feeling on the other. Grief, emerging from the heart, is buffered and supported by clear thinking. The popular saying, "Be in your heart, not in your head," can be very destructive, as the heart gives the head its true authentic direction. The head, in turn, properly assesses reality and provides the heart with rational means of expression and communication. Our heart and head are designed to work together as very worthwhile companions.
>
> ~ **Chris Saade**

brokenness. We come to be at peace with the truth of what is real. We can then learn to access more love and passion from our tears, all the while knowing the peace that comes with respecting what is real. Through the intimate and respectful knowledge of grief, the passion and peace of love are joined. This union of the fire of passion with the calm water of peace is the deep well of an astounding creative power.

At this time in history we are facing tremendously serious and frightening challenges to the Earth, democracy, and humanity. We need open-hearted leaders and citizens who are willing to generously offer their passion in service of peace, democracy, others, animals, and the Earth. This will happen only if we come to know our grief, respect it, talk about it, and befriend it. It is vital that we claim our destiny as brave-hearted souls, keeping our heart open and discovering the power and liberation that can be wrought from the struggle and suffering that is an inherent part of our existence. It is time for us to reclaim the full dignity of our humanity and the fullness of our human experience.

A culture that does not heed the collective grief of the land is imprisoned in its vanity. Individuals who have not learned to befriend and be proud of their wounds are lost in the superficial. The experience of grief frees us from this superficiality and vanity which make physical appearance and social posturing paramount. Meaning is not, and never has been, about appearances and body shapes. "Good looks" are something manufactured by mega corporations to manipulate consumer spending. The overemphasis we see today, for example, on clothing and excessive working out, is distracting individuals from their quest for meaning, high ethics, and an authentic sense of pride and service. While of course there is a place for personal aesthetics and self-expression and the importance of physical exercise, what is *most important* is the profundity of the heart, the mind, and the larger vision we pursue. The investment in false facades and superficial vanity is digging the graves of our democratic culture and

I would like to share a part of my personal story with you. When I was eight, my heart and world were shattered when my parents separated, divorced, and both married new partners, all within a brief six-month period. Over the next eighteen months, my new step-mother was diagnosed with terminal bone cancer, and my new step-father (who was an abusive alcoholic) insisted on moving us 500 miles from my father and our extended family. This was a very dark, scary, and isolating time for me as a child. I felt incredibly alone and absolutely heart broken. I learned very quickly that those around me did not want to see the amount of pain I was in and were at a loss as to how they could help.

The burden of unnecessary additional suffering and isolation that are caused by the shame and repression of our grief outrages me. Sadly, we are not taught how to encounter our grief; how to find and follow our own authentic way of grieving; or how to discover the creative force, power, and wisdom that can be mined from the depths of our pain and suffering.

In the midst of my overwhelming grief, I found a great strength within me. I vividly remember sitting on the playground with a girl in my class as she shared that her parents were also divorcing. She was the only other kid I knew whose parents were splitting up in our small town in Ohio. It was so helpful to know that I was not alone in my grief. As I was sitting with her and the whistle blew for us to come in out of the bitter cold, I heard a voice in my heart-mind say, "My pain will not be vain." At a very young age, I was able to make the choice to mine my grief and discover my greatest passion—that of supporting others with their grief and heartbreak.

~ Mandy McMullen Bird

our natural environment. By embodying our full humanity, we shed the superficiality that disconnects us from our heart, authenticity, and mind, while empowering ourselves to stand for high ethical values and unleash our deepest authenticity in generous love. Befriending our grief as a real and authentic part of our humanity as well as a source of vitality will allow meaningful desires and passions to emerge from our tears and guide us into a wisdom beyond the superficial and vain.

We become human, and powerfully so, by finding the courage to look straight at what is real and allowing ourselves to feel the impact of reality. By feeling the profundity of the reality of our life, in its grief and joy, we descend into the source of the force of love in us—that force that wants to create meaning and contribute richly to the future of our planet. Fleeing the deeper ground of our feelings disempowers us and renders us dangerously superficial. It is by claiming who we truly are (i.e. beings that are in part wounded and grieving) that we discover our deeper authentic desires and the calling that defines us and enriches our sense of soul. It is the intentional, conscious, and graceful embodying of the core feelings of our heart that reveals to us our deepest heart desires. These heart desires will propel us forward, beyond the mundane and routine, into undertaking the most meaningful journey of our life.

We will revisit throughout this book how befriending the real, including the tears that come with it, makes us co-creators rather than mindless consumers and people of high ethics rather than followers of meaningless trends and small talk. Those who can weep the tears of their heart will know the passion of soul—the passion that transforms the world step by step and intrepidly points us toward the power and vision of a greater love.

A few important clarifications:

Firstly—very important—as we delve into our exploration of grief, it is critical that we understand that welcoming or befriending our grief does not mean we are embracing the *cause* of our grief. It is our natural and powerful feelings of grief that are to be honored, whereas the causes of our grief need to be named and held in their proper

I still remember vividly the time in my late twenties when I first arrived in the United States from Lebanon. I was carrying a great deal of grief—grief from all the emotional childhood abuse that my siblings and I went through, and grief from witnessing Beirut, the city where I grew up and which I loved so much, being ravaged by the ongoing civil war. I had survived it all and was rebuilding my life with determination and vigor. Yet my heart was deeply wounded by the memories, the images, the sensations, and the flashbacks. I sought out a psychotherapist, and the process was helpful. It gave me a space to speak about my sadness. However, I discovered that outside of my therapy, it was very hard to find a community where grief could be shared and respected. The church and the spiritual groups I joined approached grief with an attitude of: "Fix it, put it behind you, and be positive." In other words, "Do not have grief." Later, when I became a psychotherapist and a coach, I heard the same disconcerting story from most, if not all, of my clients.

The inability to find spaces (other than professional offices and specialized support groups) where grief could be heard, respected, and honored was extremely difficult for me to bear. It resulted in a sense of isolation at a soul level that persisted even though I had a lot of friends and social connections. This also aggravated my anxiety and led to moments of deep dejection. I was grateful I found a space for my grief in therapy; although as a trainer of therapists, I can sadly say that many therapists are not taught the deep soul value of grief—how our tears are the source of our passion. But grief should not be hidden away in therapy as though it is a disease! Our grief should be part of the dignityof our humanity, equal to hope and joy. It should be honored as an aspect of our beautiful and creative vulnerability. I later realized that not only is our personal grief shamed by the culture at large (including

(Continued in next box)

most spiritual communities) but that our collective grief also tends to be shunned. The grief of Black Americans, American Indians, Jews, Hispanic immigrants, Palestinians, refugees, the LGBTQ community, women, and so forth, has been systematically silenced and denied. This very difficult period I personally experienced impacted me profoundly. Fortunately, I learned how to use my pain as a source of fuel for my passionate desire to help noble souls with their own grief.

~ Chris Saade

containers. From this perspective intentional grieving requires that a distinction be made in how we hold and respond to what wounds us. Wounds inflicted by the givens of our existence (for example: our mortality, the mystery and uncontrollability of life, the fragility of our physical bodies, and that we and others are limited and partial, etc.) need to be accepted as unchangeable realities. On the other hand, while we honor our wounds, the oppression or abuse that harms us or those we love must be unequivocally resisted, rejected, and condemned. Throughout this book, when we speak of befriending, honoring, or being proud of our grief and woundedness, we are talking about our authentic, natural, intelligent response to being wounded.

Secondly, when we speak of mining and transmuting our grief and discovering its gifts, it is essential to acknowledge and honor that there are wounds and losses that are deeply tragic and cause irreparable permanent damage on both individual and collective levels. This kind of wounding cannot be transmuted, but we can still tenaciously and heroically learn to stand proudly and with great strength in the midst of these harsh and devastating realities. This is the beautiful proclamation made by many Native Americans, "We are still here." It is the magnificent courage of war survivors, in spite of all the horror and cruelty, to choose and dedicate their lives to a path of liberation and love. It is the indomitable spirit of Black Americans, in the face of the seemingly unending ravages of racism, to keep fighting for love and justice. We offer our deepest respect and gratitude to all the brave souls who manage to keep going, keep creating, keep loving, and keep building islands of beauty in the seas of oppression. This book is dedicated to you.

Lastly, some words on pleasure. While this book is focused on the art of conscious grieving, it is so important to understand that our deep, authentic pleasure is a sacred source to be mined for its gifts and wisdom. In the U.S. and many other cultures, deep pleasure has been repressed and relegated to the halls of secrecy, guilt, and shame and thwarted into superficial numbing and distraction that drains and harms us and others. Authentic pleasure must be reclaimed as a vital source of strength and nurturance. Deep pleasure is the sacred twin of our deep pain. It is impossible to truly encounter the sharp edges of our pain if we are deprived of the softening cushion of our pleasure.

We encourage you to use this book as a tool to help free your own authenticity and ignite your passion by allowing your grief "to be," by respectfully getting to know it, and by learning to nurture and care for yourself while you are grieving or facing old wounds that have been buried.

In the chapters that follow, we will focus on removing the veil of shame from grief as well as offering effective and powerful tools that can support you as you encounter your grief and empower you to share this part of your human experience with others. In these pages you will find inspiration to free and take pride in your own authentic being and in the humanity of your authentic life story.

In this book we will explore how our grief—in its manifold aspects of sadness, anguish, disappointment, anger, or moments of self-doubt—is not the enemy of our joy. It is not something to run away from at any cost. Rather, grief is part of the canvas of an authentic life and of the growing passions of a life fully lived. We will underline the importance of the maturing process of our grief. Through befriending our grief, we can learn to mature it and express it with grace and in ways that will enrich love and relationships.

We hope that you may come to find comfort and dignity in your own beautiful, messy, gorgeous, broken, and magnificent human story. May blessings unfold before you through your joy and your grief, and may you meet your passion face to face and use your incredible gifts in service of greater love and liberation for your self, for those you love, and for the world!

Throughout this book you will see the points listed below explored and discussed. This exploration will support you in rethinking your grief, and thus empowering and enriching your humanity. Your humanity is so much fuller when you befriend the losses, the sorrows, and defeats of your life.

- **Your tears are the source of your passion!**

- Your courage to honor and experience your sorrows, losses, and defeats from an open heart can become a powerful initiation to the depth and richness of your soul. This bold engagement opens a door to greater and truer strength as well as to your core sense of identity.

- Numbing or repressing your grief will leave you with some level of depression, moodiness, outbursts of rage, and physical ailments.

- Vulnerability is part of your true soul power. When we speak of grief, we are also speaking of welcoming your vulnerability. Vulnerability is a fundamental part of your humanity and of your utmost creativity. True power and strength are rooted in authentic vulnerability.

- All pioneers, healers, journeyers, and true leaders are deeply wounded at their core. As you accept the fact that pain and grief are an unavoidable part of being human, you learn to encounter and mine your grief for its hidden gifts. Befriending your grief will burn away the destructive compulsion to control your truth or the truth of others. It will free you from the temptation to succumb to superficiality or the pressure to conform.

- The path of the heart is ultimately the path of love. Heart-centered grieving will expand your ability to feel love and to generously offer love. The connection between conscious grief and love, as well as between grief and passion, is one of the most crucial connections of your human evolutionary journey.

- Two essential requirements for mining the gifts of your grief are:

    1. Be radically honest with yourself and give up any habit of mental or emotional "game playing." Any form of lying to yourself or denying reality will blind you to your true power and will ultimately block your ability to experience love and passion.

    2. Grieve while knowing that grieving is a sign of strength and that you have the power within you to transmute your grief into greater authenticity, creativity, wisdom, and capacity to love. Never see yourself as a powerless victim. Victimization happens when you replace the power of genuine grief with a perception of yourself as a victim. Only in rare extreme cases are we fully powerless and therefore victimized. Children are definitely victimized by abusers. People can be victims of rape and other acts of abject violence, personal or collective. But in most cases, although we become partially victims in the event of oppression, we do not lose all of our power of will and creativity. We are wounded but that does not mean we lose our strength. To the contrary. The distinction between being wounded and being victimized is very helpful and empowering. We are often wounded by losses, difficult circumstances, and by the lies and manipulation of others. We can have self-empathy for our wounds and not succumb to a victimized mentality. We can know that from our tears a greater passion will emerge. We can be proud of our tears. You shall see throughout this book how the denial of your grief on the one hand, as well as a victimization mentality on the other hand, leaves you weakened, tragically

disconnected from your heart, and deprived of the wisdom, humanity, and passion your tears can offer you.

- There is an intimate relationship between an honest experience of your feelings (especially grief) and the development of an intelligent and creative mind (an intelligence far beyond mere shrewd smartness).

- A sustainable romance depends on the genuine sharing of (and listening to) each other's vulnerabilities, wounds, and grief.

- The same is to be said about a loving and effective parenting. It is dangerous to children when their grief is minimized, left unheard, or not respected. They build up a destructive sense of shame around their wounds. They come to aggressively blame themselves for their grief. They can be free of shame only if they are mentored into the wisdom that all human beings get wounded, at all ages, and that our existence includes sharp-cutting swords as well as opulent gardens of flowers. Children grow in great strength and self-respect when their wounds, pain, and grief are heard, validated, and honored.

This book is divided into two sections. In *Section One,* we will deeply explore and develop the sacred relationship between *grief* and *passion.* Coming to understand the inseparable connection between these two pillars of the life force will provide you with a tremendously strong and supportive foundation as you travel through your grief journey. In *Section Two* we will guide you through the model, *7 Steps Toward the Power of Grief and Hope*SM. These steps are designed to be a coaching companion for your journey and will support you in walking through both your immediate wounds and struggles as well as older griefs that are still with you. From the caves of your sorrow, you will learn how to mine the jewels of your passionate creativity and passionate vision. Developing these important skills will expand your heart, enrich your soul, and fortify the strength of your spirit.

Please remember that although the seven steps are presented in a linear way, they are also circular in the sense that you might go through them in a different sequence at different times; you might go from one to another and then back again. Each step of the model we have presented contributes to the journey of heart-centered grieving. Following the steps one after the other helps you move very powerfully through the process. These steps build on each other, but sometimes you might need to do the steps in a different order. Do what you are ready for and desire. Sometimes you will find yourself doing some of the steps simultaneously; trust your own process. Any one of them might be appropriate for a given moment. Think of them as parts of a whole; trust your wisdom, your needs, and your own pace. It is a process that must not be rushed. When you are in the midst of the shock of your loss and are struggling with acute pain, nurturing your heart and honoring your grief is foremost and fundamental. This is often the time to shed your tears and let your pain speak. Just know that beginning the act and process of honoring your grief plants, in that very moment, the seeds of an even greater love and a larger vision of your service to the world.

It is important to honor all the steps of your grieving process. There are no short-cuts. They will all support you. They will build the strength of your spirit and expand your wisdom and soul passion. The more you acquire the wisdom of a step, the more you will be ready to move to the next step, and the more you will feel supported and empowered to deepen your authenticity and unleash your heart.

7 Steps Toward the Power of Grief and Hope℠

1. Affirm Your Grief

Honor and affirm the dignity and meaningful nature of your grief.

2. Open Your Heart

Open your heart widely. Let grief expand—not close or shrink—your heart.

3. Initiation

Mine your grief as an initiation into your deepest unique authenticity, your passionate calling, and your purpose in life.

4. Paradox

Learn to fully experience the paradoxical aspects of your authentic feelings (grief and joy). Honor both rivers of feeling that flow in you—thus experiencing the fullness of life.

5. Spiritual Fortitude

Let your own heart-spirituality be the sturdy and supportive container of your grief.

6. Service

Act. Through your grief, find your most authentic and pleasurable way of serving freedom, justice, peace, and inclusion. Then take action in the world.

7. Celebration of Life

Celebrate your *whole* life—the entirety of your authentic journey—rich in losses and blessings, failures and successes, defeats and breakthroughs.

There are certain instances where we use the terms "our self" to refer to the specific and distinct entity of the "self" as opposed to the general pronoun "ourselves." Likewise, with "your self" and "yourself." These are not grammatical errors, but rather an intentional focusing on the sanctity of the individual, authentic "self" that is to be affirmed and honored.

Wherever there are spiritual references throughout the book, please interpret them in whatever way feels most comfortable to you and according to your own belief system.

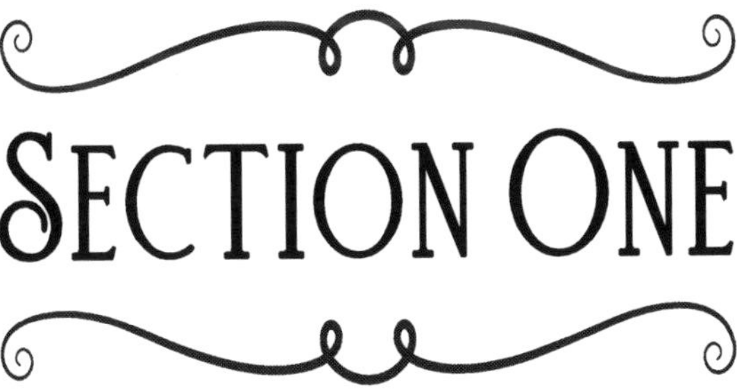

SECTION ONE

Chapter One

Grief & Passion

Before we explore the intimate and mysterious connection between grief and passion, let us take some time to define and encounter the force of passion itself.

What Is Passion?

Passion is a flow of love through the heart. Passion is the love force that becomes the deepest authentic desire blossoming from our heart. Passion is neither obsession nor compulsion, both of which are a violation of the heart. Instead, passion is a flow of energy that is congruent with the core of who we are—that is why true passion is always fundamentally an expression of love. Passion is fiery; it is also peaceful. Passion is strong, while also being vulnerable and compassionate. Passion becomes a manifestation of the truth of our being and the truth of our deepest authentic longings. It is the awakening of the daring heart. It ignites our trust in that still, small voice within. At times the voice of the heart may be soft like a dove, and at other times it may roar with the ferocity of a lion. Passion is the intensity of feeling that connects us to the great fire within. It fuels boldness. It emerges from our deepest authenticity and expresses the highest values that matter most to us. Passion helps us get out of bed in the morning and do the things in life that engender a sense of dignity, pleasure, and meaning. It channels our authenticity to flow into the world. Passion manifests itself in spite of our doubts and refuses to be paralyzed by our fears. Our fears are normal and sometimes wise, but passion is not deterred by them. Passion goes after the very things we never thought we could do.

To live passionately is to live in love with the noble and good in the world, with the Earth, and with other beings of heart. Passion is a love that flowers in spite of the absurdity of the human condition. When we allow love to move through us, we discover that our heart is stirred by a sense of care and empathy for others whose own struggles have dignity. There is nothing more beautiful than a heart aflame with love. There is nothing more beautiful than the intensity of love that is passionate whether it reveals itself as gentle and compassionate support to another or as unsubdued advocacy for justice. Passion expresses itself in many different ways, but it is always about a heart that has been touched and moved—a heart that has become aflame with the creative force of love.

To live in love awakens us to a level of understanding, a level of perception, a level of strength, and a level of courage that is beyond the normal. To be in love reintroduces us to our true self. We come to know who we are beyond the mundane, beyond the false social limitations, and beyond the injunctions and commands of the authoritarian structures around us. We discover that our wounds do not diminish us. For it is in our wounds that we find the strength of creative passion. There is a great deal of freedom in passion and there is a great deal of generosity. We discover that within our spirit there is a tremendous connection between our own authentic self, the authenticity of others, and of the Earth itself. We also discover that within us is an immense love and care for peace, for justice, for inclusion, for solidarity, and for freedom.

A heart aflame with love is an open heart. It is committed to allow passion to flow freely yet in partnership with reality and rationality. It is a heart that cares about other hearts and the soul of the planet. It is sensitive and aware of the needs of others. The heart that is open, awake, and seeking, wants to give generously and wants to enter into the great dance of life. It acknowledges the inevitability of fear and doubt but does not allow either of these to stop it. A heart that is awake and alive wants to experience life to the fullest, this includes loss, love, and beauty.

Those whose heart is aflame with love want to celebrate life even though life also brings pain and grief. They want to celebrate who they are because they can feel the pulsation of the whole Universe even in their vulnerability and in their wounds. They feel that profound sense of fulfillment that comes from being authentic in the world. They are driven to share the joy of being alive. They come to learn the deepest meaning of the word "love." They come to touch the immense magnitude of the power of love, and they manifest that power.

This manifestation of the power, passion, and pleasure of love is brilliantly displayed by a woman from Australia who went to Iraq twenty years ago and adopted not one, but two little boys who had lost their limbs. Neither of them had legs, they only had portions of their arms. This woman adopted them and raised them with immense love. She raised them to become beautiful young men who believed in themselves and knew that they were capable of living life passionately. One of them participated in a national singing competition. He sang *Imagine* by John Lennon. The entire audience was in tears and the judges deeply moved. Backstage his mother was listening, and his brother was clapping with arms that had no hands. It was an amazing expression of the beauty and the strength of the human heart when it is aflame with love.

Another example comes from the First World War. It is depicted beautifully in the movie *Joyeux Noel*. French and German soldiers were facing each other as enemies in the trenches of that brutal and bloody war. It was Christmas, 1914. The German soldiers began to sing "Silent Night" across the trenches to their British enemies. At first the British thought it was a trick; then they realized it was not. Soon they were all out of the trenches singing Christmas hymns together. These soldiers who had been fighting each other, who had been taught to hate each other and trained to kill each other, came together in a great embracing. This is why hearts aflame with passion are so essential in today's challenging world. We are facing great crises and our heart needs to be moved, to become aflame, to expand and experience the full miracle of peace and unity that only a loving and passionate heart can achieve.

Passion, in any of its forms, is a literal life force. It is a physical experience felt throughout the soul and the body. It pulsates through the veins. It is the heartbeat of life itself. We can feel and sense the energy of our passion. When we are open and awake to our feelings, when we allow ourselves to feel fully, and when we are not numbing ourselves in one way or another nor rejecting who we are because of our wounds and necessary failures, then, we can connect to the profundity of the human heart. We can hear our inner being, and we are drawn to the deepest wells of meaning in our life.

Through our grief we come to ask ourselves essential questions. Questions that are crucial to the emergence of passion: "What am I most curious about? What is most important to me? What do I care most about?" and especially, "What calling is arising from my heartbreak?" It is through such questions that the life force surfaces with new and bold choices to support what matters most to us. Risks are taken. These risks can sometimes look foolish to others, but it is through them that our life takes on a new design and opens itself to true passion in this world. Our passion then creates a concentration of energy that is like a funnel harnessing a broad spectrum of energy into a very precise focus. We know from old mystical traditions that focusing energy into a single point creates a powerful shift. This amazing dimension of passion comes from feeling the Earth, the Universe, or whatever is most sacred to us, within our own heart. It is the experience of something much greater than, but also part of, our singularity. Thus, a creative force becomes present in us—its expansiveness, its desire, and its propelling will to bestow our authentic gifts and try to make a difference in the world. When we connect with the mystical aspect of passion, we begin to feel at a cellular level that we are inhabited by a greater force, and we become more at one with the Earth and the Universe.

Passion is power, and it must be lived intelligently, ethically, and in the service of love. These are the boundaries of passion. It is a life force that must be used for peace, for justice, for solidarity, for healing, and for transformation. The power of passion is a gift that we have been given at birth as human beings. This birthright has long been celebrated throughout history and literature. In the myth of King Arthur and the Roundtable, Arthur was a young boy who was called to become King. But first he had to find the legendary sword Excalibur which happened to be firmly embedded in a stone. He had to intentionally search for the sword and extricate it from the stone. When he did, Excalibur became his life force enabling him to build, with Queen Guinevere and his faithful knights, the kingdom of Camelot. Excalibur would only surrender itself to one with an open, vulnerable, and authentic heart—an open heart truthful about its wounds, its longings, and its love. And it was only by approaching Excalibur with his passion and vulnerability that Arthur was able to claim his power, pursue his calling, and bring his dream to life. This is what we have at our disposal—the powerful life force available to a genuine and broken-open heart. Today our humanity is continuously eroded by systems of domination whether religious, social, economic, or political. We are exploited by commercial superficial trends and fads, and our sense of importance in the world is severely diminished. But when we experience our heart's true passion, we experience ourselves as strong and creative and much more powerful than the limits we have been conditioned to accept. In pursuing the passionate life, we come to fully know who we are as truly empowered human beings.

We all experience this feeling of empowerment when we fall in love. When we have a passion for another individual, suddenly we feel like we can conquer the world. There is something very real about this. First of all, we feel our passion, and secondly, we connect with the beloved at a much deeper level. This experience of being passionately in love is not limited to romantic love. It is the same experience when we feel passion for an important project, passion for bringing more justice to the world, or passion for standing against oppression. It is this same experience of passion that widens our imagination, deepens our love, and gives us a sense of renewed potency and potential.

Human beings are an incredible life force. With all the crime and heinous acts of violence and cruelty that have existed throughout history, the human heart and its capacity to love miraculously persist. We keep falling in love—with others, with the Earth, with animals, and with all the wonders of this world—and we go to great lengths to protect and care for what we love. These difficult times require and need our willingness to fall in love with love, to fall in love with what emerges from our broken hearts, and to risk feeling *so deeply* in love that we remove all the barriers and obstacles that get in the way of our loving and acting through love. By falling in love with love, we can plug into the life force of passion and do whatever we are authentically called to do in order to leave our ripple effect in this pond of life. The great philosophical and spiritual traditions have a core common teaching: love is what helps, heals, protects, and transforms. At this time in history, the Earth needs human beings who are willing to risk greatly and allow this passionate flow of love-energy to move through their hearts and out into the world.

Passion is also falling fully in love—falling in love with those who reside in our heart. It is falling in love with the animals, who are our kin, and with nature. It is falling in love with our cities and communities. And it is falling in love with the struggles of human beings for greater dignity, justice, human rights, and for greater participation in the democratic process. We must fall in love with the human longing for peace and justice. It is from this ceaseless flow of love that we can take a stand for the Earth and for its people. We know that the Earth is in great danger: We know that the senseless disparity of income is threatening economic stability around the world and causing suffering for billions of people. We know that children need to be protected whatever their socio-economic status. We also know that unless we protect our democracies and speak up for our ecosystem, the human species itself will remain in danger of extinction. It is tremendously important right now to fall in love with project Earth and to let our passion become the courage to speak for the Earth and be a voice for the voiceless. This is a time in history when every individual needs to access the passion of their heart. Every individual needs to engage from that place of passion—our very lives depend on it!

Grieving from the Heart

Loss is always difficult—the loss of a relationship, the loss of friends, the loss of a beloved parent, the loss of a job, the loss of health… And losses brought on by war or collective tragedies are extremely painful and often traumatizing. All losses are a part of the difficult reality of life, and grief (be it in the form of sadness, anger, or anxiety), not numbing, is the appropriate response to loss. Grief is about courageously facing the truth of our existence. Denial does not help because denial leads us to lie to ourselves about reality. We have to live with our wounds, gracefully and wisely. We have to learn to respect these wells of energy, passion, and vision in us.

Learning to grieve from the heart opens and expands us. Dignified grief becomes a vessel of greater love in which the heart's propensity to love grows exponentially. This ability to love, and to fall in love with, the human journey is what Heaven on Earth is all about. When we learn how to grieve, we can then learn how to be truly joyful. As we learn to grieve, we learn how to call on passion from an open and expanded heart and how to become impassioned. We learn how to build gardens of beauty in difficult environments. We begin to find strength in our vulnerability (as there is always vulnerability within true strength, and strength within vulnerability). By developing the skills of grief, we indeed acquire great abilities and wisdom.

The blessings that come into our life arise from love and through love. The more the heart is exposed to and faces the reality of its own truth and the reality of the truth of the world, the more it grows in love. Grief is an acknowledgment of the losses that we as individuals have experienced and are experiencing, as well as those that we as a world-community are going through. The world needs us to look with open eyes at the losses and the dangers we are facing and to increase the strength of love—to become creators through love. When we allow our tears to generate authentic dreams, when we allow our tears to become empathy for others, when we allow our tears to become a sense of oneness with animals and the Earth, then we transform ourselves and our communities through a profound and seasoned love.

Grieving is a complex experience. Fear of deep pain and suffering is natural for us as human beings. We do not want to hurt, and it makes sense that we are afraid of having our heart battered and broken. We literally feel our emotional heart aching in our chest. We feel the intensity of that pain throughout our entire psychological system and throughout our entire body. It impacts every area of our life, and it is scary. As humans, we like to know what to expect. We like to know what is coming next and how things will end. It is natural and human to be afraid of opening the book of our grief because there is no last page to read that assures us of a particular ending. We do not know where our grief is taking us. Yet the truth is, it takes us to a place we have never been before—it takes us home to the heart of love.

It is always our responsibility as humans to prevent suffering wherever and whenever possible, to remedy situations that create harm, and to do the best we can to minimize suffering in our life as well as in the lives of those around us. It is also very important to maximize joy and celebration, for these sustain and nourish us in a very difficult world. It is rational and healthy to avoid being wounded. However, skilled grieving is our natural and empowered way of responding to the unavoidable part of our existence that is wounding and full of struggle. There is no way to avoid being wounded; it is part of the human journey. As we learn how to grieve from the heart, grief becomes a contribution to liberation. It is like the flame that burns away the dross and leaves the gold. Grief liberates us from our forced and artificial assumptions about our authentic self. It liberates us from the shackles of, "You should do this," and "You must be that,"—all the commands that weigh down our life. There is something very liberating when we stand in the midst of grief. We stop caring so much about what frightens us, about guilt that has been imposed on us, and about the negative authorities who try to control our life. We start giving much more credence to what is authentic in us. This is how we grieve from the heart. We can learn to use the power of our grief to return to the home of our true authenticity and to shed all the masks that hide the naked truth and depth of our soul.

Learning how to grieve from the heart teaches us to focus on the core essence of things and thus to relinquish our attachment to form. This is a wisdom that has been taught throughout the ages. When we are young adults, many of us have dreams and we know exactly how we want those dreams to manifest. We want to get married and have a house. We know exactly how we would like that house to look, the colors in the house, the furniture in the house, and how the dog is going to behave. Perhaps we want to join an organization and we have a clear idea of exactly how this endeavor will be. We attach ourselves to these forms, and unfortunately, we can become rigid and stuck by confusing the form with the essence of our dreams. If our expectations do not take the precise form we imagine, we are unable to enjoy the manifestations. But as we mature and experience losses and disappointments, and as we learn to grieve and mine their wisdom, we start to realize that *forms* ultimately do not matter. What matters is the *essence* of what we are pursuing. As we strive for essence and disinvest from the rigidity of form, we realize that life meets our heart's pursuits, that our authentic longing is answered in its essence, and that our core desires become reality. Grief teaches us, matures us, and sets us on the path of wisdom to our heart, authenticity, and focusing on essence. When we set a course for essence and live by essence, we are rooted in the solid ground of what truly matters most to us. It is enriching to live freely and to discover that it is our tears which free us from our stultifying rigidity and often allow us to dance life ecstatically.

Painful experiences and losses come into our life no matter what. We can either choose to emotionally shut down or we can boldly use the losses and the intensity of the grief as a springboard into a deeper knowing of who we really are and the essence of what we want to create. Grief comes to us; we do not have to chase it down. But when we access our wisdom to welcome and encounter our grief, we choose the open-hearted and heroic perspective that illuminates the sacred in our life as well as the calling toward liberation and love.

Authenticity demands that we respond naturally to the reality of life. We respond with joy when we experience beauty in life: the beauty of love, the beauty of tenderness, or the beauty of a child running toward us and hugging us… the beauty of flowers, the beauty of trees, the beauty of water, or the beauty of mountains. Joy is part of our intelligence. So is grief. When we see somebody hurt, when we are hurt, or when we see groups of people put down because of their race, religion, sexual orientation, or socio-economic status, we are heart-broken and angry. When we witness children abandoned to a painful fate, our appropriate authentic response is sadness and often tears. Outrage is also part of our intelligence. So is peace. All of these feelings are the gifts of life and evolution. They are some of the qualities of being human. We learn to welcome and practice the full paradoxical array of our feelings. To be able to feel deeply is a great gift. We must never allow our feelings to be shamed. Our vitality and strength come through the energy of these feelings. They guide us where they need us to be, provided that we experience them deeply, encounter and express them with skill and grace, and dedicate them to love and high ethics. It is not feelings that disempower us but the pettiness (or the superficiality) of the container in which we sometimes hold them. For grief to offer its gift of intelligence, we must honor it as one of the aspects of human genius as well as dedicate its tears to love.

There is a real problem with the spiritual philosophies that teach us to *always* be positive, happy, or peaceful. In doing so, they contribute to the numbing of our authenticity. They dehumanize us and attempt to turn us into robots. We need to be encouraged to feel all our feelings; only then can we mine from them our unique creativity, service, and passionate pursuits. Grief is the companion of any genuine life and a wellspring for authentic and passionate action. When we attempt to only focus on positive thoughts while the authentic reality of our life demands from us to be outraged, sad, or anxious, then in the name of "positive thinking" we control and suppress the truth of our being. This throws us into inauthentic experiences of our self and an inauthentic presentation of our self to the world.

The deeper spiritual experience leads us to realize that from grief great blessings can be born. We must never lose faith as we are grieving. We must also refuse to surrender to victimization. We must grieve as empowered and mature human beings, never as victims. We must learn to hold our wounds as honorable, keeping our eyes on our lionhearted determination to extract greater meaning and love from the ashes of our pain. Grieving from the heart means grieving with courage, strength, maturity, and faith. It means standing in the authenticity that liberates us and guides us toward more soul and a larger, more powerful heart.

Grief and Passion

There is a unique and intimate relationship between grief and passion. What is that relationship? Why are these two seemingly divergent emotions not only related to each other but inseparable? The connection between grief and passion cannot be severed. The reality is that often our encounters with grief introduce us to our greatest passion. And it is our greatest passion that fills us with the strength and vitality to face and hold and respond creatively to the heartbreaking challenges we face individually and collectively. In the breaking of our heart and the shattering of our illusions, we are guided into the intensity, the seeking, the longing, and the wisdom of our calling. We are awakened through our "dark nights of the soul" to the deepest longings of our heart. We come to meet who we really are at an ever-deeper level. We cannot fulfill our own destiny and live its passionate heeding without learning the art of feeling and transmuting our great heartbreak.

It is in this mystical and very paradoxical way that undamming our deepest authenticity and grief can introduce us to our passion. It is very important to grasp how our wounds, like our successes and triumphs, are our wells of energy. Our wounds and our grief release a great deal of creative energy which is at our disposal. If we encounter our grief consciously and with respect, the energy released can become a powerful, and often exceptional, passionate creativity. Encountering and mining our grief enables us to go for the impossible, to dare to love boldly and generously, to seek out the depth of our authenticity and edge of our dreams, and to take a stand for justice in this world. We can use our grief to help us open up to these great longings and callings of our heart. Our passion is ignited by our suffering. To love passionately—to live passionately—is to know existence in its quest for meaning and sacred hopes. Without passion we limit our self to an experience of life that is tremendously diminished and often depressing. It is our very authenticity—living a life that is congruent with what is true, and real, and natural for us—that gives rise to passion. Grief, in addition to joy, is an integral and genuine part of living. Life and the world have overwhelming beauty to offer, but there is also great pain. This is the way the world is. We see great devastation, pain, and suffering in the world and also experience it in our own life. We are called to mine a passionate calling from our suffering and show up worthy of the meaning in our suffering!

There is indeed immense beauty in the world—beauty that produces joy and pleasure in our life and gives reason for celebration. There is also pain and sorrow. If we are blind to beauty, we lose our sense of direction and hope. However, if we run away from grief, we close our eyes to a big part of what is real and true—and in the process, we lose our passion. It is only by accepting what is real and facing what is true that we encounter the full magnitude of life. When we understand this, we can give birth to our passion. It is like standing on a mountaintop and looking out at the world: we see beautiful forests and stunning vistas; we see the sunset with its colors illuminating the skies; but we also see the devastation done by hurricanes, forest fires, as well as the destruction from rampant logging and overdevelopment. When we acknowledge *all* that we see, when we have the courage to see the *whole* picture, then we truly are able to be intimate with all that life is—the good, the difficult, and the ugly. If we refuse to see the broken trees or the areas burned by fire, if we refuse to feel our grief, then our constricted and defended heart will be unable to fully see the beauty in our lives. We will not feel the passion for Planet Earth. Passion is awakened in us through seeing what is real and experiencing what is true. Grief is part of what is true in our life. Our passion is born out of the commitment to open our eyes and to take in the complete fullness of life.

We want a meaning-filled life, and it is the passion of the heart that leads us to such meaning. Passion fuels us with the grand intensity of longing and fills our heart with deep feelings and strong vitality.

And *all* feelings, when experienced at their depth, are life-giving—including grief itself. We cannot experience the passion of life moving through us without experiencing grief. Although grief hurts and sometimes brings us deep pain, it also brings us again and again into the humanity of our own heart, our own authenticity, and connects us with the longings of the world. Grief is a great initiator that teaches us what it means to be fully human. Our losses create a thirst in our being for more—a thirst to seek and *find* more meaning. Through our grief, we come to know how sacred life really is.

It is grief that ignites our deepest passion; and it is through such passion that we come to fully recognize meaning and beauty in life. By trusting our grief, we discover the profoundly intimate relationship between our grief and our longing to be awakened—our longing to live a passion-filled life. By honoring our grief, we come to love ourselves in our vulnerability as proud and sensitive lovers and powerful wounded creators.

Many of us long to be awake and fully alive. We are hungry for experiences that connect us to our deep being, to other human beings, and to a greater Power—the great mystery of life. We want to know that our stories matter and that our life is not in vain. Despite all of the things that do not make sense to us, we want to know that there is value, meaning, and something sacred about our own individual journey. We want to experience the ecstasy and beauty of life through being fully alive. Waking up to our passion means that we are willing to pay the price of being fully real without pretending, hiding, or minimizing our experiences. It means not accepting the superficiality that robs us of the passionate life. This is why it is so essential to respect and honor our deep grief as well as to honor and mine our deep joy and pleasure. Allowing our deepest feelings to flow wakes us up to the truth of our being, to our authenticity, and to our power. It allows us to shake off social falsity and to meet our true and authentic self. This is what ignites our heart and leads us into a passionate life.

There have been many times in my life where I have felt very afraid and consumed with grief. There were years as a child and teenager that I lived in fear daily. My mother had married a man who moved us 500 miles away from our extended family and my father. This was before the internet and mobile phones, and long-distance phone calls were very expensive, so we had little contact with our family several states away once we moved. My stepfather knew this would be the case. He was a Dr. Jekyll and Mr. Hyde type of character; a violent abusive alcoholic who, when sober, was as charming as could be and looked like Robert Redford. I spent many days in absolute fear and sorrow. I remember feeling at times that there was very little hope that we would ever be able to get away from him. My mother had grown up in a very loving family and was completely out of her league with this man's tactics of manipulation and abuse. She felt helpless, guilty, and covered up in shame. (She eventually did gather her courage and got help to get us all away from him.) I was very protective of her and my brother. We never knew which nights my stepfather would be coming home, and if he would be sober. And what a mean drunk he was! Somehow though, there was a fire in my spirit, and I was determined that this man was not going to win. I wasn't going to allow him to make me feel small or hate myself—which is what abuse does to its victims. One night after he and my mom had a horrible fight, I demanded that he open the locked door. I could no longer hear my mother and was terrified of what he had done. For some reason, he did what I demanded and opened the door. My mother was laying knocked-out on the floor. I thought she was dead and was screaming at him that he'd killed my mother. Thank God, she came to from my sobbing and we spent the night in my room with the door locked. The point of this story is that no matter what I have faced in my life, I've always known and chosen to plug into the passion that lives within my

(Continued in next box)

own being. I've chosen to keep hope alive in me and growing up I read stories of great heroes like Frederick Douglas and Harriet Tubman. Those inspiring stories strengthened and emboldened my spirit. I refused to allow my stepfather or his abuse to win. I knew I was loved, and I was going to love my own spirit no matter what! I knew there would be better days ahead, and I wasn't going to miss them. I was determined that his abuse would not shut down the light inside of me.

~ Mandy McMullen Bird

At this time in history, the human species is facing one of its greatest challenges. It is dealing with the threat of its own extinction. The ecological devastation that we have inflicted on Planet Earth is taking us to the brink of disaster. The economic divide between the poor and rich is getting much more extreme; our democracies are being besieged and often dismantled and we do not know if they will survive. Fanaticism is developing in the world, extremism is becoming rampant, and terrorism is raising its heinous head. In these challenging times, and as children of the 21st century, we are asked to undertake a leap of consciousness that will give us the courage to stand for the highest ethical values that we believe in and espouse. The Earth is asking us to claim our passion—the passion of love, the passion of care, the passion of protectiveness. The children who are suffering throughout the world, and the children of the future, need us to awaken fully to our loving passion so that our unified voices will help restore peace and usher in a vision of justice. Only this will prevent our extinction. Yet we can only advance in growth and wisdom if we come to feel our own wounds, the wounds of humanity, and the wounds of the Earth. If we refuse to honor our tears and the tears of others, we will numb our heart and mind. If we do not mine the great gifts of our collective wounds, we will forgo the wisdom that can take us to new horizons of possibility.

On a global level, a wise passion for the Earth and for democracy is essential for the survival of the human race. Passion is about maturity of the spirit; it allows love to seize us with its vision. Passion is about knowing our limitations as well as the limitless force of spirit within us. Passion is about dancing life into being and celebrating the grandeur of who we are in our essence as humans through our vulnerabilities and despite the profound challenges we face as a global community.

Passion that arises from the heart leads us to act in ways that we never dreamt possible and to be creative in ways that humankind is only beginning to discover. The creative response to our greatest challenges is crucial. We must avoid both negative responses that plunge us into despair and positive naïve ones that blind us to the seriousness of the threats we are facing. Instead, we need a creative response that will unleash our authentic passion to find new solutions to old festering problems in every area of life: within our families, friendships, and communities, as well as in the areas of science, philosophy, and politics. Yet this high level of bold creativity will not happen if we do not respectfully embrace our grief, wounds, and defeats. There is an undeniable and close relationship between grief, on the one hand, and passion and creativity on the other. Grief intensifies our thinking, focuses it on ultimate priorities, and releases the high creative energy of the mind. Through heart-centered grieving the heart opens up to the edge of its authenticity and to its utmost creativity.

The passion of the heart leads us to imagine a world beyond the structures and schemes of domination, control, exploitation, and rabid competition. Passion brings life to the words: love, freedom, peace, justice, inclusion, and compassion. Yet passion, creativity, and joy, *as well as* grief, are all part of our full authenticity. By saying "Yes" to life and to all that is part of life, we come to the ultimate realization that our tears and grief are the source of our greatest heart-passion and of our most daring visions of love, care, and solidarity.

How does our grief connect us with the struggles of the world?

Grief visits each person's life through their own unique experiences, carving their individual path to their own passion and calling. It is an experience that brings with it a sense of direction, meaning, and purpose. But feeling grief is not complete on its own. We have to go on a seeking journey with grief—a heroic journey—before grief can deliver its full message about who we are and what we are meant to do in this world. When we embark on this journey, we find that it is our grief that encourages us, inspires us, and leads us directly into the core of our passion to make a difference in the world. Who better to love and serve the world than those with broken-open hearts? No one does it better than those who have experienced heartache and suffering. Our pain as individuals is in partnership with the pain of the world. It is through this understanding that we are able to respond with a vision of healing, transformation, and peace. Our vision of service is born from our greatest wounds. This is when the intimate connection between us and the world arises in sacred partnership.

All great social causes are propelled by people who personally know the pain of injustice and oppression. It is those who allow themselves to feel the full grief of their heart's suffering who become the social activists of great change. Mexican American, Cesar Chavez, was an immigrant who experienced the pain of working with very little protection and very few rights. He was abused many times by land owners, and he was paid very little. He courageously and creatively drew on his long-suffering experiences to develop a transformative vision that became his life's work. Through activism and organizing, he created the National Farmworkers Association, which later became the National Farmworkers Union. He brought tremendous advances into the lives of millions of farmworkers. His birthday, March 31, is now celebrated as a state holiday in California, Texas, and Colorado.

He is just one of the many global activists for social justice whose lives were shaped by heartbreak and suffering.

In *Section Two* of this book, we offer a seven-step guide to explore an empowered, heart-centered path through the grief journey. These seven concrete steps support and honor our authenticity and guide us toward liberating our authentic self from depression-of-spirit, powerlessness, and enable us to manifest the heart through love-in-action with others and the world. In the first step, we will discuss also the difference between clinical depression and the depression-of-spirit, and how grief by itself does not lead to any form of depression.

Chapter Two

Elements of Passion

There are several foundational elements needed to ignite and sustain passion. These elements help bring us into closer contact with the life force and with our own power to encounter the fullness of life and love with all their beauty and struggle.

Heart

Living from an open heart and daring to follow the guidance of our heart is essential—that is, to do what Waldo Emerson said so beautifully and succinctly, "Obey your heart." See the heart as the temple where the ultimate resides and from whence life flows. It is vital to make clear that the longings and core desires of each person's heart are sacred—in the sense that they are essential for their life and their quest for meaning and self-realization. Each of us is filled with longings and desires. Passion arises when we descend into the profundity of our longing and discover our deepest core desires. We cannot disregard the life force in our heart expressing itself as longings and core desires. These are part of our invaluable singularity.

The longings and core desires of the heart have led human beings to cross oceans, explore outer space, study the tiniest of microcosms, and continually find fascination and wonder in the great mysteries of life and love. It is truly awe-inspiring to behold what the longings and desires of our heart do within us as individual beings as well as collectively within our shared humanity. The longings and desires of our heart are the core of our true identity.

Desire is a word that can feel risky, but at its foundation it is about action. Desire is heart-inspired action that brings gifts far beyond our imagination. (*Desire* is very different from a *wish* which is a hope outside of our field of action.) We need to trust that our heart contains our own truth and that our core desires are our most precious treasures. A core desire is a life force that is intended for both us and the world. They are our guides and compass—our own personal GPS. We have the obligation to muster the courage and audacity to live from the place of the core heart desires within us.

If we do not allow our selves to feel and experience our losses, we can become embittered and hardened. We may become emotionally reactive, rigid, apathetic, and perhaps vindictive or abusive. But when we experience loss from the tenderness of our heart, from the love of our heart, then loss liberates us and guides us, through our emerging deep desires, into greater harmony with our self.

We are wise to listen to the guidance of our heart and follow it. Our mind needs to respect the integrity of the heart and support it. However, the mind is essential for naming and discerning the ground of reality in which the heart operates. The mind can provide rational and powerful tools for the fulfillment of the heart's core desire. True intelligence, strength, and passion emerge from a strong mind supporting a strong heart. Our heart must set the direction of our life, for within the heart resides who we are in our deepest truth; while the mind enables the heart to incarnate into the world with intelligence, grace, and power. The passionate heart supported by the clear mind—a match made in heaven!

Listening and following one's heart is most crucial. There is no path without the heart. There is no real human and caring culture without the heart. So many of our large corporate structures attempt to banish the heart and justify this by claiming that there is no time or space for the heart when an organization is trying to maximize profit for its shareholders. Unfortunately, this tragic phenomenon is taking place in almost every area of our society—from medicine to sales, from politics to production, and even in our education system! This is an immense mistake. It is ruining the humane interaction between provider and consumer which is greatly damaging to business as well as people. Leaders who have a true vision know better. They know that the heart and success are not in opposition, but to the contrary are strongly connected. There is no meaningful and truly creative passion without the heart!

Authenticity

Authenticity means living from the true self we already are, and not from some fantasy or false self that we erroneously think we should or must be. If the open heart is the fire that ignites and sustains our passion, then authenticity is the ground in which these flowers of fiery passion can grow.

One of the greatest tasks in life (maybe *the* greatest task in life) is to reclaim our true self—to liberate our selves from the shackles of the false selves that have been imposed upon us. Too often, we accept the demands of our false self and make them our own. We convince our mind that these demands, although they are not authentic to us, are necessary. We give in to thinking that success in life comes from doing the "correct" things—whether or not we desire to do them and whether or not they are authentic or connect us to our own genuine source of fulfillment.

The development of a passionate life is related to reclaiming more parts of our true self and realizing that our true self, is in its essence, beautiful, noble, most needed by the world, and exactly who we were born to be. We need to realize that who we are as individuals—in our heart and mind, in our body and psyche—is something extremely precious and something that has been carved through hundreds of thousands of years of evolution. It has taken the whole journey of the Universe (over fourteen billion years!) to create the stars, planets, and most recently, individuals who carry consciousness. Every one of us in our true self is an amazing entity of life—a unique, singular gem of creation and evolution.

Our journey is all about progressively reclaiming the true authentic self. It cannot be done quickly. It takes a lot of commitment and time to move toward our authenticity. But it is this journey that liberates our creative energies, our sense of purpose and calling, and our ability to fill our life with the joy that praises life, love, and the Sacred.

Our greatest challenge is to embody our true self because it is the source of our passion, the source of our profound joy, and the source of our noblest values. It is the source of our impassioned service to the Earth and to those who need their rights to be restored and their lives honored.

It is fascinating how much our culture strives for *individualism* (the sense that an individual can be completely independent from others) yet does not really support *individuality* where the true uniqueness within each person is celebrated. One of the ways that we all experience the oppression of the true self is through shame; shame tells us that who we are is not to be trusted or is not enough! It tells us we are not smart enough! It suggests we are too short, too tall, too this, too that! Shame is a tricky and oppressive force. In many families we get the message: "Do not be too different and make us uncomfortable. Do not be too unique." There is so much pressure within many families to follow the collective rules and guidelines. "Do not dare become a chef or a poet or a musician;" or if you come from a creative family, maybe "Do not sell out and make too much money." But in either case, the message is clear: "Always represent the family beliefs and ideals." We get many gifts from our families, but we each have an individual spirit and a unique voice and presence in the world. Shame within a family can pressure us to conform in ways which do not represent who we truly are.

Culturally, there is a lot invested in making sure that the individual does not step into his or her true self because doing so generates true freedom. Empowered and passionate free human beings will refuse oppressive systems and stand for democracy and true peace. It is critical that we become conscious of the forces working against our authentic freedom. In our educational institutions, for example, our young people are not usually encouraged to search for the great passions of their heart. They should be encouraged to go after what is authentically exciting to them and what will bring them a deep sense of meaning and fulfillment. This far outweighs the importance of making a lot of money for its own sake. We are often shamed if we do not follow particular guidelines and rules about what it means to be successful within our own community culture. This is a grave injustice and leads to psychological and emotional pain and disorders for the individual. We all know we need a certain level of money to survive. But we also need to feel peace within—to be aligned with our own authenticity—and to fulfill the calling to serve the world from our authentic individuality.

It is deeply saddening to see how many religious institutions encourage people to think and believe the same way. Under this influence, the importance of each and every one of us finding our truest nature as individuals gets lost. This pressure to be "the same" and fit in to these dogmatic religious and spiritual systems does not allow for the manifestation of the unique individual or its expression in the world. This is tragic. Furthermore, for those of us who believe in a higher being, the suppression of authentic individuality discourages the intimacy that the Divine seeks with us. How can we be close to the Divine if we do not believe that the Divine wants us to be who we authentically are?

Saying "No" to shame allows us to reclaim the pride of spirit that the ancient ones carried so well and so profoundly. From Greece to

Phoenicia and through the history of the First Peoples of the Americas, ancient civilizations knew how to walk proudly. But this sense of individual dignity has been taken away from us. We have been made to believe that our own authentic spirit is deficient or broken, unreliable, and untrustworthy—and in some traditions, even sinful and in need of redemption.

Shame began rearing its ugly head long ago when human conglomerations began to develop ideas of empire and domination. We can trace this to the early times of the agricultural revolution about 7,000-9,000 years ago. For the first time in human history people were able to accumulate and own a surplus of food. They were able to store their additional supplies and trade or sell them at a later time in order to gain more resources. This stockpile of product eventually allowed the development of surplus capital which then was used by some to enlist mercenaries to develop their military power. As a result, ideas of empire and domination began expanding within some people's imaginations. Such new imaginings gave rise to the Babylonian, Egyptian, and Roman empires. As time passed, we also witnessed the emergence of the French and British empires and others. Today, the United States is an economic empire. History clearly reveals a definite correlation between the spreading of empires and the propensity to diminish the freedom of individuals and impose uniformity on society.

That begs the question: how can it be that small groups of people—i.e. the leaders of empire establishments—were able to wield their minority power to an extent that dominated millions, if not billions, of people? The only way such domination of the many by the very few could occur was through making millions of people believe they were sub-human. Through belittling people's authentic sense of being, the manipulating powers of empire led people to distrust themselves or believe that they held no power within their intrinsic authenticity. Then the "powerful" ones, those who participated in ruling the empire (those who had the surplus product), identified themselves as semi-divine and as the ones who were "worthy." The rest of the population was thus deemed "unworthy." When people believe they are unworthy they lose their strength to stand up for freedom and to stand up for their democratic and human rights. It then becomes much easier for the powers of domination to control them.

Throughout time, this cultural message of unworthiness was infused into religious messages. Such religious messages taught individuals to believe that there was something fundamentally wrong with the core authenticity of their being. The messages were pervasive and attacked the worthiness of the authenticity of people from multiple angles. This voice of domination and control delivered the message: "There is something wrong with your nature. There is something wrong with the way you manifest yourself in the world. There is something wrong with your personality, and of course in addition to that, your sexuality..." The list goes on and on. These notions of "wrongness" about the core of our authenticity (rather than about specific destructive behaviors) ultimately claimed that people are born in sin and therefore cannot trust their corrupt inherent nature. With original sin the belief developed that one's individual nature had to be changed and cleansed of its corruptness. This led large masses of people to believe themselves to be defective and deeply flawed human beings. Then, the belief that they must spend their lives trying to free themselves of themselves naturally followed.

Unfortunately, in contemporary times, we have seen empire thinking, ideas of domination, and sin-based beliefs spill over into secular psychology. In therapy, in far too many consulting rooms, people are told they need to change—not merely any destructive behaviors, which should be addressed, but that they should change who they are in their genuine essence. They are told there is something wrong with them that needs to be fixed or resolved. For many, their whole life is then spent trying to change who they are. This is very different from the approaches to therapy developed by Abraham Maslow, Rollo May, Fritz Pearl, and other existentialists. These psychological thinkers proposed that therapy needs to be about a process of self-actualization in which people discover the fullness of who they authentically are. Existentialists supported individuals becoming impassioned, mature, and strong versions of themselves in service of love in the world. This is very different from the idea that there is something inherently broken in us that requires us to spend our lives attempting to change who we are (and become somebody else). The psychological approaches that adopt such self-deconstructive methods play right into the idea of shame and the belief that we cannot trust our authenticity: our heart, our personality, our inclinations, and our core desires.

Most people have not questioned the danger of shaming the individual self. There has been a complete lack of understanding or awareness regarding how such shaming leaves us unable to celebrate the unique and individualized reality of our being. There is no room within this empire ideology for people to be proud of themselves. As a result, many were unable to be faithful to the passions born in their souls and to develop their passions toward greater love and greater service.

Liberation from this history of shame is essential—essential to claim the beauty in our lives, the joy and the grief, the celebration, the passion, and the noblest ideals of our humanity. The depression-of-spirit born of this shame reveals how great the loss of our authentic humanity has been.

When thinking about the authenticity of the individual self, it can be helpful to consider the variety of animal species. All species are connected within the great circle of life, but they are also extremely diverse, and every animal has different likes and dislikes. Some like the light; others like the dark and live underground. Some hunt during the day; some hunt at night. Some run quickly; others sit still, patiently waiting. There are so many different ways of being in the

The journey of my life has been about returning to my true self, reclaiming my authenticity, becoming more natural, and learning to be fascinated by my own spirit, as well as the authentic spirit of others. As I am growing older, I am finding that in many ways I have more energy, feel lighter, and am more able to engage in the celebration of meaningful moments in life. In spite of my increased physical vulnerabilities, especially in the area of chronic migraines, I have more vitality of spirit than ever before. I carry more grief and tears over losses that have seeded my life, yet I have more strength and tenacity because I feel that I am embodying more and more what is truly authentic in me. I am not tortured by the guilt and shame of not following prescribed roads and ways of being. By becoming more attuned to what is natural in me, I feel more connected to our precious Earth, to the Sacred, and to the life-giving energies of both.

This is the whole thing about aging—it gives us the opportunity to become freer and discover a greater connection to what is natural in us. Although our body ages, we can grow stronger in our heart energies, our free thinking, and our capacity to uphold meaning and a greater sense of social and ecological solidarity. Our life force grows exponentially when we reclaim our authenticity.

Aging is a very good example of how loss and grief can be a source of blessing. There are parts of our bodies that obviously weaken; I know this. There are sicknesses that visit us; I know this too. There are limitations that grow within us. There are great losses and grief, but I also know that if I approach my losses from a place of dignity and heart, I can discover a richer authentic experience of myself. Then aging, and the losses it brings, can result in the manifestation of rich blessings for me—for us—that expand the heart and expand our ability to uphold the depth of life and love like never before.

~ Chris Saade

world, and they are all valid. Nature in all its richness and glory teaches us diversity in everything! We too, as human beings, are diverse. We each have our own particular inclinations. Honoring these natural and innate individual tendencies is essential to our authenticity and to our well-being.

Such self-honoring requires a person to lovingly embrace the stirrings of their psyche as well as accept what their psyche is *not* drawn toward. So too with our mind: to live within our authenticity is to fully accept—without judgement—what fascinates our mind and, equally, what does not interest our mind. Likewise, viewing our lives through authentic eyes also applies to our sexuality and how our sexuality expresses itself. The path of authenticity is an exploration of who we really are and who we are not—an exploration to be undertaken with great respect, intentionality, accountability, and love. To be authentic is to revere and honor the wonderfully individualized heart, mind, body, and spirit that we have each been given. It is this particular heart, mind, body, and spirit that bears the power and beauty of our true name. Each of us is so unique in the way we create and fulfill our destiny. Our creative idiosyncrasies are part and parcel of the authenticity of self that needs to be respected and honored. Passion in its depth is an expression of our authenticity and is sustained by our authenticity. Through our authentic uniqueness we experience the richness that our path provides for us, but also the losses and disappointments our particular inclinations are bound bring about—again joy and grief!

In relation to education, we have come to understand the importance of an educational approach that respects the diversity of learning styles. Howard Gardner, a developmental psychologist, Harvard professor, and author of some 30 books, has stressed the theory of multiple intelligences and demonstrated how people learn differently given the variety in types of intelligence—all of which are valid and powerful in their own way. Schools must accept that they cannot deliver the same educational approaches for every student and expect to have impactful and lasting results.

Our creative idiosyncrasies are well illustrated by using the language of archetypes. We all have different dominant archetypal instincts, and we all create in different ways. We all learn differently. Some of us, for example, are the wandering type who wander in our creativity and go from one theme to the next. We like to discover and explore possibilities and are circular in the way we create. Contrastingly, some of us are more hunter-like, setting goals and going for them with great focus. Some of us are builders building slowly, like a squirrel gathering nuts for the winter one nut at a time, and then we slowly start seeing results. And then others are sprinters, manifesting in a flash. Some of us are supporters. Some of us are pioneers. Some of us are jesters that create through laughter, jokes, and bringing a life-giving levity to difficult situations. Each of these is an example of a different type of archetypal intelligence. How wonderful it is to claim the authentic truth of our nature and to recognize the beauty in the vital authenticity of others. Beauty does not reside in good looks or commercialized fashion trends but rather in the honesty of our authenticity and the love that can pour out of being attuned to our true self.

It is indeed a struggle to give ourselves permission to feel the vital energy of our authentic identity. This is part of our task as human beings on the psychological and spiritual journey. We must commit to letting go of that which does not belong to us. We need the faith, courage, and willingness to be fully who we authentically are and to resist who we are not. This crucial freedom and authentic embodiment might demand a high price, but it is undeniably worth it. The freedom of our irreplaceable and unique authenticity allows passion to flower in us. The judging voices introjected into our head make it difficult for us to be true to our authentic self. But it is a noble fight, worth every tear and every moment of grief—a fight that enables us to free ourselves into being who we really are. By taking on this liberating inner battle, we release endless energy and a power that enables us to shift from the exhausted dread of trying to "keep it together" to a new place within us that allows the false self to fall away and who we really are to emerge and blossom. By becoming true to who we really are, we nourish our passion and bring numerous moments of precious joy into our life.

Enthusiasm

"Enthusiasm" in the ancient Greek tradition meant being visited by the goddesses and the gods. It is a choice to make ourselves an open and welcoming space to be visited by the energies of life, by the energies of the Universe, and by the energies of love—with both our tears and with our joy. It is a choice we consciously make daily to invest fully in celebrating life, to build relationships, to struggle for peace and justice, and to pursue reconciliation and transformation.

We must dare to live with enthusiastic determination. We must choose to live enthusiastically in times of joy and grief. This enthusiasm, this exuberant response to life in all its challenges, is made up of both open heartedness and wise discernment. This is essential to having a meaningful life and to be able to mine the treasures in our grief and our losses. Likewise, this is what enables us to push back against victimization. When we choose to live enthusiastically, we are saying that we may be hurting and in a lot of pain, but we still trust the creative force of life within us. There is an endless well of enthusiasm for life, liberation of authenticity, and love that we can choose and learn to draw from. This is an extraordinary power that no one and no circumstance can steal from us. It is an assertion we make in opposition to and rejection of the forces of oppression and abuse. Oppressive forces and people can and do wound us deeply, but the life-giving waters of our intentional enthusiasm can never be cut off.

Every day is an opportunity to access, strengthen, and cultivate the life force moving through us—to enthusiastically greet life in its beauty and its struggles. Regardless of our experience, be it trauma or bliss, we can elect to keep our "eyes on the prize" of the liberation of our deep authenticity and love. The force of our enthusiasm can help us extract what is life-giving and love-generating from the ashes of our suffering. Our bold enthusiasm can help us bring to light more of our authentic self every step of the way. It can fill us with the strength to rise to the occasion and say, "I will work and stand for my highest genuine ideals. I will liberate my authenticity. And, I will call forth the courage to cultivate the great passion of my heart."

The inverse is also true: we can only live enthusiastically when we are aligned and being faithful to the truth of who we really are. Pretending to be something we are not or forcing ourselves into a life that simply no longer fits our deepest authenticity makes it very difficult, if not impossible, to access the well of enthusiasm. It takes tremendous energy to maintain the false self. Instead of embracing our own individuality, we can get so involved in making up a false social self that our energies are drained. By hiding and denying our authentic self, whatever the reasons we use to convince ourselves, we are left with very little energy to be enthusiastic. Alternately, living aligned with our authenticity allows us to move through life with the passion, exuberance, love, and excitement for fulfilling our destiny; protecting those we love; and caring for this beautiful blue planet which we call home. When we embrace our true self, all of a sudden, we have the vital energy of spirit that invites us to breathe in every sunrise and end every day with a sense of strength and being at peace. But we have to choose enthusiasm. It benefits us to intentionally call it forth.

Connection

Remembering our connection with our precious Planet Earth and with the struggles of humanity (solidarity) is essential for cultivating passion. Isolation paralyzes us and drains us of inspiration. It is about recognizing that we are truly one with the beauty our Earth and one with the struggle of every noble-hearted woman, man, and child in their quest for dignity, justice, and peace. The struggles of others must be seen and honored as *our* struggles.

We cannot live authentic lives without feeling our belonging to the greater story of humankind and without experiencing our rootedness in this Earth. We are of this Earth and not here to live a life separate from the struggles of others and the needs of our eco-environment. If we isolate ourselves from this bigger story, we wither, and our passion dies.

We are needed. Our experiences and the heart wisdom we have gathered, combined with the beautiful idiosyncratic nature of our authentic being, are needed. There are people who need us. There are projects that need us. The Earth needs us. There are animals that need us. There are causes that need us. Many rely on us, just as we rely on others. We benefit from and are strengthened by others' advances in authenticity and freedom. They enrich our lives. Those who are building an inclusive democracy need our voices. This is an intimate and intricate relationship. Passion does not flourish if it is not connected to a larger meaning outside of our own individual life. It is so essential to understand and feel that we are not walking around as individual islands in competition with each other. Of course, our individual needs are important, but we can only meet them through an expanded circle of interconnection. We need each other's authenticity. That is the reality. The more we experience ourselves as part of the collective striving for greater freedom and justice, the more our heart will know the fire of passion. Participating in the larger struggle not only brings us greater meaning, it fuels the flames of our passion. As we offer our passion, we receive from others, and the circle goes on!

If we numb out—avoiding our feelings and our grief—or succumb to the social pressures to pretend we are not in pain, we lose the opportunity to allow a birth to emerge from our grief. Grief is a most precious womb. Grief helps us learn about who we are and what matters to us most in the world. Grief teaches us how we want to spend our time, where we want to give our energy, and who we want to spend our time with. Grief, by humanizing us, teaches us about our highest values and our hopes. Grief assists us by helping us learn what ignites our inner fire, what excites our spirit, what calls to us, and how we can best give back to the world. This is why it is so essential that we take the time needed and invest our efforts into our grief journey. If we do not, if we avoid our grief, we lose the vital opportunity to mine the wealth of our authenticity and its passionate calling. We miss the treasure. We miss the discovery of our authentic truth and we miss the deep revealing of our life's individual meaning and purpose.

> After experiencing the death of a loved one—whether it be a spouse, a child, or a beloved friend—many clients have said to me that the things they thought mattered no longer matter at all. Hundreds of people have said this to me over the years. What matters is the preciousness of life and giving back to others. When grief enters our world and loss visits our life, we experience a death, an ending, whether it is the ending of a dream or the actual physical loss of a loved one. At the same time, it can become an awakening. Our wounds can become an opening within our authentic being. We are no longer caught up in the trappings of superficiality when significant grief and loss come into our life. This is one of the ways grief gifts us and why I feel so passionate about this message.
>
> **~ Mandy McMullen Bird**

It is through experiences of loss and grief that we are prodded to realign our will with the core desires of our heart and the truth of our authenticity. Will is a powerful force but sadly it is often disconnected from the authenticity of our personality and heart. When this disconnection happens, a split occurs within the individual. Our will is effective when it emerges from our authentic heart's desire and passion. We can suffocate passion if we try to will or force our spirit to bend toward a preconceived idea (even a good one!) of what we want our desire to be or think our heart should want. In contrast it is a beautiful moment, when in the throes of loss and grief, we listen to what our heart intensely desires, and we come to that gentle and peaceful place of restoring the original harmony between the authenticity of our being, the genuine longing of our heart, and the powerful force of our will. In this state of harmony, our will becomes a most powerful force that serves (rather than controls) our authenticity and heart longings.

The authentic experience of grief and loss can unify the desires of our heart with the great hunger and yearnings of the world. By being in touch with this unity, we are able to create unexpected miracles through our losses and grief. Such miracles, while often manifested through pain and suffering, paradoxically reveal that pieces of heaven can be achieved on Earth when we live authentically from the heart with passion and celebration and with the genuine truth of our grief.

One paradoxical marvel is how consciously engaging our heartbreak and loss can open us to deeper love and solidarity with others and the world. It is our grief that so often compels us toward compassionate action. Our grief, not in spite of our pain, but through our pain, can set in motion a deeply compassionate and justice-seeking desire to serve others who are in pain. Out of empowered grieving, great strength can be engendered. We have seen this time and time again. The Susan G. Komen Foundation was founded in honor of a sister who died of breast cancer. Through this organization's efforts, millions of people have been served through education, research, and awareness. Mothers Against Drunk Drivers was founded by a woman who lost her eighteen-year-old son in an accident with a drunk driver. Similarly, the television show responsible for helping to apprehend over a thousand violent criminals, *America's Most Wanted*, was started by Adam Walsh after the abduction and murder of his son. Walsh went on to lobby and fight for missing children and victims' rights, appearing multiple times in front of Congress.

The emergence of such organizations and programs is not a coincidence. In the wake of tragic grief and loss, we often witness the birth of important humanitarian organizations. We see movements dedicated to peace, freedom, and justice spring up around the globe. We hear stories of countless hours of compassionate work being offered on behalf of those who are struggling. As mentioned previously, our deep grief, if intentionally felt and embraced, humanizes us. Such felt grief opens the gates of the heart (which is crucial to mention again and again) and through these gates we are gifted the opportunity of entering into empathetic solidarity with the pain of others and our world. There is a very real relationship between our own experiences of grief and loss and the passion to serve others. There is an innate urge within conscious human beings to create from (and through) their losses and give back to others who are also grieving. We want to reach out and wrap our arms around others and say, "Hey, I am still breathing. You can also draw strength and vision from your wounds. I have learned how to be with and move through my pain and my suffering. And, by the way, I have learned a lot about myself. I am blessed, and you too can actually find joy again by generously sharing your authentic gifts and making a difference in the lives of other people."

In my coaching work I have been blessed to witness many meaningful and enlightening experiences with clients. One such beautiful experience was with a woman who did high level administrative work. She was very well paid and highly recognized and honored for her work. But at the end of the day, she felt uneasy and dissatisfied. One day she came home to find her dog very sick. She rushed her dog to the animal hospital, but it was too late and the dog died the same night. She shed profound tears and decided to take

(Continued in next box)

three days off to grieve the loss of the dog she adored. She notified her work that she would be gone for three days and would take a leave of absence or whatever it took. She then spent those three days reviewing photographs of her dog and crying her heart out. On the third day she invited her friends to a goodbye party for her dog that had been such a faithful companion. She went back to work for a couple of days but by the weekend it really hit her that she did not want to continue with her job. It was her spirit speaking—a spirit laid bare by a grief that became anger: "I do not want to continue doing my job. It is not my passion. I do it well, and I am remunerated well, but it doesn't fulfill me. My dog died. I do not want the instinctual force in me to die along with my dog. I want my passion back." She was startled by her own response and realized, "My God! This is the gift my dog has imparted to me. It is as if my dog is telling me: Do not let your spirit die. Reclaim your spirit." The following Monday she sent a letter of resignation. By choosing to make space for and listening to her deepest authentic truth, she realized that she no longer wanted to be in an office. She remembered growing up on a farm in her youth and how much she loved all the animals. She decided to venture back to a farm-life where she could raise animals, especially horses, and she would be able to house a lot of dogs. She pursued her heart-calling and continued to listen to her authenticity. Eventually, she developed a weekend program for physically challenged children to come and spend the day with the animals on her farm, so they could be supported and nurtured by them. She was greatly gifted by mining her grief for its gold.

~ Chris Saade

On our planet there are millions of people offering jewels of wisdom and comfort to others who are grieving their losses. This is one of the great blessings of the paradoxical impact that grief can have on our lives—individually and collectively. It is neither simple nor easy to face grief with courage and openness when there are big parts of us that are tempted to withdraw and shut down emotionally. We have to remain bold and firmly planted in the intention that no matter what happens in our lives, we will remain authentic, strong, and open-hearted beings who are ready to give back to the world through the wisdom of our losses. It is tragic when individuals numb their heart so as to avoid feeling grief. They might remain smart in certain ways but lose their profundity and their soul intelligence. When we desire to proudly embody our humanity, we honor and ennoble our grieving heart and become aware of a compelling force that will bless us and bless others more than we can ever imagine.

When these foundational elements of passion are brought together in our journey of grief and loss, a powerful dynamic circle of passion is created: ***heart, authenticity, enthusiasm, and solidarity***—intricately interwoven and working together to strengthen passion and sustain it.

I had an experience of standing up to shame that I will never forget. I was participating in a personal leadership training workshop, and within this group of more than twenty people I spoke about something I was struggling to accept about myself. One person within the group said, "You have to basically tell shame to jump in the lake." Everyone in the group screamed from the top of their lungs, "Jump in the lake! Screw you Shame!" I will never forget that as long as I live.

Those powerful voices screaming with me, "Go away shame!" Since then I have had many fewer struggles in my life around shame. I may have doubt. I may have worry. I might be anxious about doing something new. But shame no longer has the same power over me.

Growing up, I certainly experienced shame in my family, and I definitely experienced shame in the church where I was a member. I

(Continued in next box)

know how difficult it can be to say "No" to shame. To say, "Get away from me!" But here is my commitment: I will, as long as I am breathing, allow myself to be who I am, because who I am is needed in the world." I encourage you to say that to yourself as many times a day as it takes and to imagine that your brothers and sisters around the world are supporting you by shouting out against shame. When we set our authentic spirit free and know we are beloved by the Divine and that who we are is a gift to our own spirit, to God, and to the world, there is no longer a place for shame.

~ Mandy McMullen Bird

Growing up in an emotionally abusive family, I learned very early on that my natural authenticity was not acceptable and that I was supposed to try to be so many other things for so many people. I was taught to be one way for my father, and another for my mother, and yet another for my uncles, and this and that for my teachers, and yet another persona for the church. I tried to please everybody. In my late teens and throughout my twenties I became so exhausted by the end of each day from trying to meet all these demands to be obedient, to appease, and to please. Many ancient spiritual teachers tell us that enlightenment is not about adding much, but about letting go—letting go of all these false selves so we can enter into the simplicity and the power of our truth—our authentic self. This reminds me of how nuclear energy is created. It is not about expansion. It is created by descending into the very small point that then creates an amazing expansion of energies. Our true self is that source of energy, while our false selves (however well intended) are energy vampires.

~ Chris Saade

Chapter Three

Global Grief as a Call to Immediate Heart Action

The global situation at the beginning of this third millennium is grave and most dangerous. Many are questioning if the human race can survive the great crises it is facing.

The first crisis is ecological devastation: our violations of Earth's natural systems are leading to what over ninety percent of the world's scientists describe as the heating of the atmosphere resulting in climate change. Such change is shifting weather patterns which will affect everyone, everywhere, especially the poorest among us.

The second crisis is the absurdly widening economic divide between the mega-rich and those who are working multiple jobs and struggling to survive. The current income disparity is an untenable gap never seen before at such a wide level throughout our history. In addition, worldwide, the middle class is dwindling and melting away at an unprecedented speed.

The third crisis is the danger to democracy around the world. This crisis poses a very dire threat to civilization as we know it. Our democratic systems are being besieged by groups and individuals who want to see authoritarianism, if not a form of fascism, restored.

The fourth and final great modern crisis is the rise of extremist ideologies in both religious and secular thinking which are resulting in ever-increasing bloodshed and terrorism.

These are very serious crises we face today. We cannot afford to close our eyes to these threats affecting us all, whatever our financial status, race, or creed. Now more than ever, our world needs those who are willing to open their hearts to feel the grief around these issues and take specific action to help restore ecological sustainability, peace, freedom, democracy, and a wider sense of justice.

How we respond to the vital needs of our planet will determine if we are to make it into the future as a civilization and as a human race. People from all over the world are beginning to feel anguished around these crises. This grief needs to be affirmed. We need to feel the Real—feel what is actually happening to our precious Earth and to human civilization. This grief can become the sanctified womb of great birth if we allow ourselves to embrace it and stand in its truth. Unless we can feel it, we will keep closing our eyes to the precipitous threats we all face. Our collective denial is a most dangerous and ominous enemy.

This global grief is leading many in the world, particularly the younger generations, to put their hand to the plow and make a difference by going for love-in-action. We are seeing millions of people from different countries, religions, and philosophies starting to make a real difference in the world. Through love-in-action, they are saving forests; cleaning rivers; rescuing animals; and getting involved in nonprofit organizations that work for peace, human rights, inclusion, minority rights, and social justice. These are people who are feeling their grief and allowing it to awaken their passion for Planet Earth and their longing to make a difference in the world.

As we come to partake in the global grief of our world, we have a chance to join hands with sisters and brothers from all faiths and all countries who are saying we need to love the Earth, we need to uphold the best in our fellow human beings, and we need to love all of those who are noble of heart and who are struggling. As we come to feel this global grief, we can then stand up and direct the force of our will toward transformation. Our future, our very survival, depends upon this happening. When we face what is Real, carry the grief without succumbing to despair, and know that we have the power in us to love and make a difference, we awaken the deeper dimensions of our being. We awaken the sacred in our heart and unleash the immense and unbounded strength of love.

It is easy to feel overwhelmed when we hear these words about global grief and the threats to our planet. While it is extremely important to fully acknowledge the seriousness of what we are facing, it is also tremendously important to remember the significant historical breakthroughs we have experienced in our world. We need to be grounded in both of these realities, so we do not lose our resolve. There are so many historical events and evolutionary changes that have expanded human rights and freedom from oppression. Today, it is easy to take such achievements for granted. For those who have lived through these struggles and through difficult moments before change occurred, the challenges seemed insurmountable. Yet, the power of everyday heroes and brave groups of citizens has brought about change. It is essential that we remember it is always the individuals who go against all odds who precipitate change. They overcome apathy, complacency, and hopelessness. They act on behalf of what is just and attend to what is in front of them. The reality is that we each have our piece of the puzzle to contribute, our unique way of serving through love-in-action. Each and all of us have our unique and authentic part to play within the grand orchestra of humanity.

As our global grief has the power to awaken each individual heart to its wider capacity for love and service, so too does this grief carry the power for collective cultural awakening. A new wave of engaged spirituality is ushering in a new way of thinking and acting that is underlining the importance of individual freedom and authenticity brought together with the generosity of love-in-action.[1] In addition, this arising wave, this embodied spirituality, is bringing us to the realization that we are in a very real solidarity with our Earth, animals, and everyone of noble heart who is struggling. Thus, along with the awakening of the authentic individual, there is an awakening within us related to understanding how we intrinsically partake in the global longing and struggle. This parallel awakening is leading us into deeper self-knowledge and a deeper knowing of ourselves as a species and a community at a collective level.

Will we awaken collectively? Will we allow love to turn our grief into passionate action? Will we allow ourselves to love the Earth enough—to love our human journey enough—that we will take a stand and do what is needed to save ourselves from the destruction we are seeing around us? We do not know the ultimate answers, but we do know that the journey forward poses two critical questions that must be addressed: "Who am I in this individual body, this heart, this mind, and this psyche?" (In other words, "Who am I as an authentic and unique human being?") And secondly, "What are the ethical qualities that define us collectively as human beings?"

We are beginning to realize, how much we share energetically with all those who choose the path of the heart and how much we are interconnected with the Earth, with the Universe, and with one another. We are beginning to realize that this interconnection is deeper and wider than we ever thought. We have also come to understand that this sense of oneness is not only a theory or a vague spiritual concept; oneness is social, economic, and political solidarity with others. It is realizing that what others go through impacts us at a cellular level and within our psyche. Our health—be it mental, physical, or emotional—is linked with the suffering and soul joy of others. There is no way we will come to address the urgent needs of our world without recognizing

[1]For a more in-depth exploration of this topic, please see Chris' book: *Second Wave Spirituality—Passion for Peace, Passion for Justice*

our connection with the longing of others for freedom, authenticity, and a life of meaning, as well as our gut-level oneness with our home, Planet Earth. We are beginning to awaken to the realization that others live in us and we live in others. This integral connectedness is something that serious spiritual teachers have taught throughout the ages, great social reformers have understood and proclaimed, and now science is beginning to confirm for us.

The Areas of Authentic Oneness

There are important areas of oneness which we are beginning to grasp. The first connects us with those of our ancestors who worked and struggled to expand human rights, democracy, and greater freedom for the human family. The ancestors who stood against the tyranny of empires. The ancestors who said "No" to concentration camps and "No" to the fascism that divided humanity into the rulers and the "worthless." These ancestors—these women and men of great heart, ability, and courage—whatever their limitations and mistakes, live on in us. They are part of our psyche. We are not born into a *tabula rasa*, a blank slate. We are born with the memory of these ancestors who are seared in our mind and in our psyche. Their longings and their courage live on within us and we are one with their collective human vision.

Second, we are realizing that others' struggle for justice, dignity, freedom, inclusion, and peace (whether in our town, our country, or in foreign lands) is intimately tied to our own everyday struggles. When people of heart suffer, we suffer. When people are oppressed, we are in pain. Many of us are not conscious about this, but as we do become conscious, we realize how much we feel the suffering of others in our body as well as feel others' true joy.

A third area of oneness is the oneness with all children. The prayers of suffering children, the most innocent among us, are imprinted strongly in our heart and in our psyche. They are calling us to action.

When children scream their hunger and pain to the skies or pray for deliverance from the wars that are terrorizing them—these prayers reverberate deeply in our own heart for we are guardians and protectors of the world's children. They break our heart open, so the great passion of compassion can flow through us. We are beginning to hear the cries and the prayers of suffering children.

A fourth area of oneness is our belonging to the Earth. We are feeling the effects of the desecration and pollution of forests, rivers, and seas. We feel the malaise in our own body. We literally feel sick about what is happening to the Earth itself—and to the animals. Many people know the suffering of animals as if it is their own; this is not just merely a concept, but something felt so strongly that they are compelled to do something on behalf of the survival of animals on our planet. We know that we are part and parcel of the Earth. We are not irrelevant, disconnected inhabitants of the planet as we are led to believe, but rather we are integral co-creators of the breath of the Earth itself!

In summary, when we realize both the collective grief and collective joy that live in us, we become receptors for great wisdom and inspirations that propel us to act. We begin to have revelations of what we need to contribute, specifically in response to our world's impending crises. We begin seeing. We start understanding. We begin acting in the spaces we inhabit to make a difference where we work and where we live. We feel grief and joy and allow these to birth a new consciousness that unites the personal and the global. This consciousness, awakened through the collective and expressed through the personal, is all about the heart aflame with love and the intelligence of love.

The other side of our awareness of our oneness with the sad and tragic realities we face is that we are also collectively intertwined through the joy, pleasure, and hope of transformation. Whenever and wherever democracy is restored, greater justice is sought, or wars cease for some of us, we are *all* lifted up and empowered by these breakthroughs. At such times there is a great sense of joy and celebration, and we feel it on a personal level even if it does not impact us directly. An example is when the Berlin Wall was demolished. Worldwide, people celebrated with great joy even if they had no direct connection to Germany. We are intimately tied to that joy and celebration, just as we are connected to the pain and suffering brought on by the building of the wall. We are one with all heart-centered people—our sisters and brothers in the world trying to make a difference. We are one with the millions involved in nonprofit and humanitarian organizations and with all those who are becoming voices for the voiceless and performing acts of compassion and solidarity around the world.

It is most powerful to see that our own story is woven into Earth's story. It is most powerful to know ourselves as global citizens who can make a difference in our own communities by generously offering our own authentically flowing gifts to the world. Such a vision of our unique and liberated individuality participating in the collective story of our world's struggle for justice and freedom brings great nobility to our grief and hope. No matter what our losses, we are given the opportunity to see our sacred place in the story of humanity—to see the noble worthiness of our caring heart and how the planet herself is inviting us to engage, each in our own natural and authentic way. We are global citizens. Through this recognition we access our power. We feel our own heartbreak and allow it to connect us to the heartbreak in the world. It is our courageous response to this heartbreak that allows us to access our passionate power to do the work that gives expression to our particular authenticity and destiny. As we follow the calling of our heart, we discover that we participate in the creation of meaning as well as find a sense of profound personal fulfillment. In both personally and collectively difficult times, we can (and must) transmute our pain into vision and allow our grief to birth powerful, richly creative, and life-giving responses to the challenges we face.

I am thinking about a dear friend who, throughout his adult life, experienced a great deal of grief in relationship struggles. As he moved through his adult life, he did his personal work and allowed himself to feel his own pain and his own suffering. He awakened to what was going on in the world, to what was happening in the rain-forest, and to what was happening to dolphins. He became completely fired up about what was happening environmentally to our planet and spent much of his time giving back and educating people about what they, as individuals, could do to make a difference for the environment.

This is very inspiring to me and a great reminder that any of us who have had our heart broken and impacted by loss, regardless of what the loss is, if we are willing to keep our heart open, we are then sensitive to the concerns of others and to what is happening to our planet. This is the energy that is needed in the world. Each of us in our own way can make an impact by paying attention to what matters to us and elevates our passion. Like my inspiring friend, we can put our tears into action, into love, and into service for the needs of the Earth—ultimately, the needs of us all.

~ **Mandy McMullen Bird**

Opening up to the full expression of our humanity changes our life. It changes how we view our suffering, and it changes the meaning of our suffering. We become empowered and inspired. We claim our active citizenship and our individual role, be it small or large, in the healing and reconciliation of our planet.

We are called to be giants of love and giants of love-in-action. We are called to feel the world in joy and in sorrow. We are meant to feel the love that is our birthright and our richest legacy. We know that our liberation is one, our joy is one, and our grief is one. When we realize that our individual suffering is actually connected to the suffering of others, it brings a whole new level of dignity to our grieving process.

It helps us be patient with ourselves and understand why we hurt so deeply at times and in ways that we may not clearly understand. Personal grief and the grief of the world are deeply interconnected. We are not isolated islands grieving on our own. Understanding this allows us to feel greater patience and respect for our grief and for the grief of the world. We are all intricately woven together.

The oneness of grief unites us. When a person loses a loved one, they feel the immense grief of losing that person, but they also can tap into the collective grief of everyone else who has lost someone in their life. When a person loses their job, they feel the incredible grief of losing that job, but there is a profoundness to their grief that can allow them to also feel the suffering and the pain of others who have lost their jobs. When someone is struck with an illness, they grieve the loss that that particular illness is ushering into their life, but at some level they are also feeling the loss, pain, and arduous load that every person bears when they are struggling with illness. Our grief is one. Grief can reveal to us our profound unity.

As we allow ourselves to feel our grief, honor our grief, and see our grief as sacred, we learn to share it courageously—both on an individual level and on a collective and political level. Our tears can cleanse us of our paralyzing resentments. Our shared tears become sacred and holy water which fills the chalice of reconciliation and the activism of love. We learn to share our heart gracefully without hiding any part of it. Such transparent sharing empowers us individually and also greatly enriches our relationships. Relationships need authenticity, openness, and vulnerability to thrive. A rigid "positive" approach to relationships sucks the air out of our authentic connections to each other. Authenticity, generosity, and respect for vulnerability are the tools that buttress romantic relationships as well as families.

In mystical terms, our deep grief is God's grief; God grieves through us. This supreme expression of oneness reveals an intimate relationship that is a grand mystery. Many spiritual teachers throughout time and

> In the work I have done in negotiation and reconciliation—between different religious groups like Muslims, Christians, and Jews, as well as in my work coaching couples—I have seen that what allows people to bond, even when holding a great difference, is sharing their grief. Through grief, an amazing humanization of the situation occurs, a great softening. All of a sudden people see the other in a whole different light. They become united through the sharing of their sorrows. I saw this between Palestinians and Israelis who would aggressively debate for hours about who was right and who was wrong, but when they began sharing their grief about how their families have suffered or how they have lost loved ones in the war, all of a sudden empathy, understanding, and relationships were created. As personal griefs were shared, we saw people reaching out from different parts of the room and hugging people they had considered foes moments ago, saying to them, "I know what you are going through."
>
> They were touched at a profound level that no mere intellectual debate could reach.
>
> ~ **Chris Saade**

history have reminded us that we are the ones who act on behalf of the Divine. We are the hands, the feet, and the eyes through which the Divine incarnates. Likewise, we are grievers for the Divine. Our grief is a powerful expression of God's love and is a call to action—an invitation to be servants and co-creators of love and solidarity. As servants of love, we are able to feel the grand importance of experiencing our grief as the grief of the Divine. The mystics say the same for joy. Awareness of this relationship underscores the importance of the role we each play, being called to do our part to help hold the great grief (as well as the great joy) of the world. So often when we are grieving, we feel very isolated and alone. Those inclined toward mysticism recognize that the Divine is grieving through them, they realize that they are never alone in their grief. They teach us that when we grieve, we are holding the tears of God and that when we hold hope, we are holding the loving hope of God for humanity. This allows us to claim our luminous place in the grand human story.

When we experience our feelings at this deepest of levels, we connect with energies that are universal and cosmic in nature. When we allow ourselves to feel our grief at this level—where the personal intersects with the global and our own individual tears blend with the tears of the world (and of the Sacred)—great loving and creative forces, immense in their potency, are unleashed within us. We participate in forces that are shaping the human psyche to learn to love on a grand scale and to show up in the world in the freedom of our authenticity, in love, and in courage. This is the great participation—the oneness of the individual with all the amazing powers that exist in the Cosmos, the Earth, and in the unfolding of human history.

Chapter Four

Saying the Great "Yes" to Life

The Importance of Celebrating the Wounded Spirit

We are all wounded spirits. We walk on this Earth carrying our personal wounds and our wounded history. We all know or remember wounds arising from abuse in families or oppression by political, religious, or economic institutions that crush the freedom of human beings. We weep, broken-hearted, as the memories of the horrific wounds of slavery, the holocaust, and refugee camps flow through our mind. We walk slowly through the heaviness and anguish of death and sickness. We are all affected by the ecological violation of the Earth. We all carry deep wounds within us, and these wounds are a part of our sacred nobility.

To celebrate life, we do not wait for the (nonexistent) unwounded person within us to arise. We celebrate through our woundedness—we celebrate our own wounded spirit, and we celebrate other noble-hearted wounded spirits. We come to truly love ourselves in our hurt and hurting humanity—seeing our magnificent dignity. Although the spirit within us is powerful, we all have tremendous lacks and important vulnerabilities. None of us is totally whole or void of lacks, and this is why we need each other in genuine and profound friendships, community, and relationships. We are all lacking in some way or another. We were made to be powerful partial beings. Our highest creative intelligence comes from our partiality! Our authentic lacks and vulnerabilities do not take away our strength, to the contrary, they increase it. It is like looking at a magnificent horse running through the wind, and then seeing that its leg has been injured and has a scar. The skin shows its vulnerability and its fallibility. Yet we look at that horse and we are in awe of its power and magnificence in its woundedness. Its wound is part of its glory and beauty. As human beings, we must understand how the wounds we carry do not detract in any way from the vivid colors of our spirit. Actually, they add to the richness, depth, and character of our being. They humanize our spirit and make it more tender, empathic, and receptive—as well as sturdier. Our courage is not wielded in steel perfection, but in real soul.

There is no reason to wait to celebrate our own wounded spirit or those of our children, partners, friends, and families. There is no reason to wait to celebrate the wounded spirit of our fellow human beings who are trying to serve, make a difference, uphold greater peace, drive reconciliation, or build justice in the world. There is no need or reason to wait. There are, in fact, very good reasons to celebrate right now, *today,* with our tears, our brokenness, our losses, and our gifts and blessings. We can celebrate with both the successes and the failures which are intrinsic parts of our progression through life. The great "Yes" is the voice of a wounded spirit responding to the vastness of the ocean and the wonders of the sun that always rises and sets in splendor. It is the wounded spirit feeling its connection to life and offering itself genuinely in service and care.

When we are wounded, it is too easy to feel that there is nothing to celebrate simply because we have been taught to avoid talking about our wounds. We are made to feel ashamed of our lacks and never mention our defeats. We are encouraged to put on a cheerful "positive" mask and do our best to hide and deny our pain and struggles. Most of us have experienced being put down because of our vulnerability and have remained ashamed of it. We have been conditioned to believe life is either all good or all bad. This is a serious mistake. Currently, the prevailing positive thinking ideology does not want to recognize that life flourishes in the paradox of gifts and lacks, strength and wounds. Our vulnerabilities are part of the fullness of our life journey and we have every right to celebrate our struggles and our defeats as well as our triumphs. We have the right to celebrate the totality of our life, to honor our wounds and celebrate their meaning.

It is difficult, given the way most of us have been conditioned, to realize that we have every right to celebrate the fullness of our journey. It can feel odd as we transition our thinking into grasping the reality of our right to celebrate and the benefits of celebrating the totality of our own being and life journey. We have been deprived of the awareness of our power to mine our wounds. Our wounds bring us gifts about our authenticity and offer us greater freedom and love for our selves, our beloveds, and in the world. If we wait to celebrate until we get it all together, the stars are aligned, and we are perfectly happy, that day will never come. We can fake it, but it is not real. Resilient strength arises from the winters of our humanity. And all that waiting means we are missing out on the beauty and nourishment of being fully alive—alive in our grief and joy!

There is a lot of cynicism today about our humanity, about our democratic system, and about the dignity of our own individual authenticity. The dangers we are facing are very real, yet it does not help anyone that cynicism has become trendy. Cynicism is very dangerous because it leads us to disconnect from the heroic spirit of love within us. Cynicism becomes a poor excuse for not getting involved or for failing to show up for the Earth, our democracies, the children, and the animals. Our acts of valor, done out of love and compassion, keep building possibility in rather impossible times and bringing constructive changes for humanity. It is crucial that today we reject cynicism. Building democracy, building communities, and creating the best that we can imagine for our humanity, is the triumph of the human spirit.

We cannot let the horrific experiences of our history, even ones from the recent past, detract us from the fact that many amongst us have never ceased their work to bring social and political reforms and usher in an evolutionary consciousness. These determined open-hearted ones have created charters for freedom and justice, developed medicine, fought against slavery, and built democracies even when they were impossible dreams. They have spoken for children's rights, progressed toward more equality for women and LGBTQ freedoms, and fought for the well-being of the Earth and animals. Yes, there is still a lot to be done—a great deal—but we cannot discount how amazingly powerful and beautiful it is that the noble-hearted ones of our human race have constantly re-birthed themselves from the ashes, like a phoenix, and reasserted themselves in service of life and love, even on the heels of horrific events and through abominable conditions.

To feel empowered in our life stories, it is essential to understand and celebrate our journey with its wounds and unavoidable defeats. All of it is an important contribution to the larger human story. We must relearn to celebrate not some perfectionist fantasy about wholeness but the real wounded-hero experience—both our own as well as the wounded-heroic aspect of humanity. When we do, we show up with a love that will not abate and a passion to love that cannot be stopped.

The Essential "Yes"s and "No"s Proclaimed

There are essential affirmations that our spirit can determinedly and heroically express regardless of the circumstances in which we find ourselves. Millions of people around the world choose to say "Yes" to life and love even under the most harrowing conditions. They stand and scream a great "Yes!" with all the passion of their hearts—a great resounding "Yes!" to the meaning of their existence on this planet. It is a "Yes" that calls love and strength into our heart and leads us to show up to our story and to answer our calling to authentically and generously love in the midst of all the storms and obstacles we face!

However, it is also important to remember that there are great "No"s that must be asserted to protect a vital and real space for the great "Yes"s to exist. These sacred "No"s emerge from the reality that there is a great struggle that exists between the forces of love and the forces of oppression. (There are some perspectives that believe we are meant to accept or transcend *all* of existence including abuse and oppression; we believe this is a very dangerous approach that prevents an empowered clarity of what we are fighting *for* and what we are fighting *against.*) The essential "No"s include refusing, rejecting, and condemning *all* forms of abuse and oppression (such as racism, sexism, homophobia, and xenophobia to name a few). It is also critical that we say "No!" to any shame or diminishment of our authenticity or truth of who we are and who we are not. We must say "No!" to the destructive temptations of superficiality, conformity, lying, and control. Liberation and love also require a firm refusal to adhere to familial or cultural injunctions that malign our authentic personality, true passions, or calling. Bravely asserting these liberating refusals makes space for the affirming "Yes"s presented below. May you feel empowered and proud as you say "No!" to that which is oppressive. This courageous clearing creates the space for what is true and life-giving!

The Passionate "Yes" to Life

The passionate "Yes" to life is essential if there is to be transformation and empowerment independent of our circumstances. We say "Yes" to life by rejecting oppression and by affirming that our life has a meaningful calling worthy of pursuing. The young Anne Frank died as a Jewish victim of the holocaust during the Second World War. She ultimately was a victim of the holocaust, yet during her two years of hiding prior to her arrest, she made the decision to write and share her thoughts and the intense passion of her heart through her diaries.

This young girl has inspired generation after generation through her passionate "Yes" to life in spite of harrowing circumstances.

Another well-known example is Harriet Tubman and the Underground Railroad. Her fearless choices over and over again during slavery helped free her enslaved brothers and sisters. How important her great "Yes" to life was for so many during that very dark time in history as well as for us now and for generations of the future. The enduring legacy of the great "Yes" lives on because of the strength of her and many others' courageous and decisive actions.

Dr. Martin Luther King, Jr. had a very clear awareness of the danger he was in on the last night of his life. When he gave what would become his final sermon, Dr. King acknowledged the danger of potential hate crimes against him and the untimely death he might face because of his outspoken call for racial and economic justice as well as his position against the Vietnam War. The next day he was assassinated. He knew the risk, but nothing deterred him from continuing to proclaim the great "Yes" to life in order to serve the higher vision.

Of course, not all assertions of the great "Yes" to life are tied directly with public issues or life-threatening dangers. Yet those that are related to a potential loss of life, such as the examples above or from incurable diseases, et cetera, are powerful examples of how individuals choose to affirm life no matter what! It is essential that we recognize that our own "Yes" to life is needed by future generations. Young people look to their elders to help pave the way as our ancestors did for us. Through each authentic assertion of "Yes," we shepherd others, and are shepherded ourselves, to remain present to life and affirming life.

Learning to say "Yes" to life is important for all of us and especially important for the younger generations. We are seeing a staggeringly tragic number of suicides and life-threatening addictions plaguing young people who were not mentored in how to discover their authentic calling. In a world that so often sends messages of conformity and hypocrisy, young people can become discouraged, confused, and cynical toward life. It is our ethical responsibility to set the example of saying "Yes" to life: to live our authenticity, to follow our heart-passion, to honor and learn from our grief, and to embrace the joy of love. In doing so we inspire young people who need examples of mature individuals who are willing to push back against an oppressive system that is telling them not to be their genuine selves, not to feel the depth of their feelings, and not to listen to their heart's calling. Such modeling for our young people matters deeply for humanity. One of the most life-affirming things we can do for our children is to affirm their authenticity as precious and unique and their wounds as noble. We need to remind them that life resides in the fullness of their journey! And then, going one essential step further, we empower our children tremendously by supporting them—from a very young age—to discover and develop their deepest passion (which is so closely connected with their pain, grief, and wounding). Support and encouragement in this regard empowers children to assert their own full "Yes" to life.

The Passionate "Yes" to Love

The great "Yes" to love involves an awareness of how love can and needs to flow through an open heart in spite of the violence and the pain that is a part of our ongoing experience of life. May we remember that in spite of horrendous events in human history, love did not disappear from the human heart. Think of the First World War and the Second World War and the millions of casualties; think of slavery, the holocaust, the massacre of indigenous populations, and of course other tragic and devastating happenings, yet we still desire to pursue love. Love is a most mysterious flame that cannot be extinguished. Love is the source of our greatest achievements. But we have to say "Yes" to love. We have to find the courage and the determination to embrace it and embody its stunning energy.

Love exists and persists in the face of suffocating religious rigidity and political authoritarianism. These oppressive systems disregard freedom and authenticity and disparage our need for heart-to-heart connections in our personal and professional interactions, to maintain an active democracy, and for a viable relationship with the Earth itself. Despite it all, love endures! Love is the greatest force in all of humanity. Love is seen every day in simple moments of tenderness and intimacy. It appears in a moment of holding the hand of someone else and saying, "I am here for you." Love is also the hunger for freedom and justice for all. The bright and shining force of love never sets. The sun sets at the close of each day, but love? Never! To say the great "Yes" to love is to realize that we are part of a cosmic story of love—quantum in nature and beyond our full understanding. Yet love is the story that writes itself through us.

Saying "Yes" to love is the source of an amazing power. Mothers and fathers know this when they have children with long-term illnesses requiring daily care. They might both have full-time jobs, yet, despite the demands of their work, they are devoted to their child and give of themselves beyond what they could have previously imagined possible. Those who care so deeply say "Yes" to love, and love says "Yes" to them. They know and feel that they are partaking in a communion with something larger than themselves, something sacred and most beautiful.

When we forget to look at life through the eyes of love, there is very little left to be seen. But when we view life through the lens of saying a passionate "Yes" to love, we realize there are stars in the firmament around us. We recognize that heart-rich neighbors, strangers, and noble people from diverse backgrounds can present themselves as actors of love in our life. Daring to experience the passionate "Yes" *to* and *of* love leads us to hitherto unknown frontiers of ourselves. Love stretches our imagination. It shows us that the real treasure is a heart that has learned to bond with others and knows how to abandon itself to the generosity of loving. Love gives us the experience of touching the heart of others and having our heart touched—an invaluable experience. Passion in its real sense is love brought to its utmost limits.

The Passionate "Yes" To Our Own Unique Authenticity

Affirming who we are and standing courageously for the truth of our authentic self is no small deal. Our life depends on it. It is a choice between being lost in the masses of followers or becoming our unique true self. We each have the singularity of our individual landscape crafted in a unique way, and we share in the longing to free and self-realize our authenticity.

Yet *to truly love ourselves* is not possible unless we utter a passionate "Yes" to the full authentic human being that we are. We are called to say a passionate "Yes" to the uniqueness of our own self with our particularities and idiosyncrasies, richness and vulnerability, sturdiness and woundedness. We serve our selves and the world when we proudly affirm our authentic personality which is gifted and lacking, ever resilient yet anguished, and a creator of successes but also a bearer of important defeats.

Severed from the ground of our authenticity, our spirit can neither survive nor thrive. As we begin to protect the particularity of who we are, we say a strong "Yes" to the authenticity of our true self. We understand that love requires us to give most generously to our selves and to others, to not hold back, yet always to offer from the truth and wellspring of our authentic gifts and desires rather than from forced guilt or contrition. We need to remove our selves from situations that disparage our authentic being and heart-truth, and when our authenticity is respected to offer our gifts with utmost generosity.

Fidelity to our natural authenticity sharpens our mind—the mind becomes clearer and its vision more potent. Only when we align our selves with our authenticity can we break free from the confusion of a mind split (and battered) between what is genuine in our selves and the false, artificial facades imposed on us. Authenticity of heart, nature, and personality are the elixirs for highly effective intelligence. We are asked to wholeheartedly choose to be who we are. We are not asked to change ourselves, but rather to mature our individual nature and offer it for love and service. We have to resist the shame that pollutes our singularity of self. To be different and unique is not a problem—it is a luscious gift. As we descend deeper into our authenticity, we become better able to hold the paradox of our unique individuality combined with our union with others in hope and destiny.

No matter our faith tradition or non-faith tradition, allowing ourselves to embody the deepest authenticity of our own spirit—and to be at the same time in solidarity with the Earth and the world—is a profound spiritual journey. It is in many ways an ecstatic joy to incarnate our own authentic spirit and go into the deeper layers of who we are: our greatest griefs and joys, our cherished dreams and longings, our noble failures and successes, and our passionate heart-calling. To claim the fullness of who we are, to inhabit our own skin, and to allow the incarnation of our spirit in our body, is a joy to experience and behold. In this magnificent expression of authenticity, the Universe, the Sacred, and the beauty of our own spirit all merge together—this is a place of ineffable ecstasy of soul.

The liberation of our spirit leads us gradually to this sacred place of harmony and unity with our own true self. The more of our authenticity we claim, through our grief and with our grief, the more we experience the ecstasy that comes with being who we truly are in our uniqueness and our humanity. Native Americans have a beautiful saying that expresses this idea: "When you have lived in dignity and integrity of spirit, then every day is a good day to live and a good day to die." It is the realization that standing in our authenticity is key to each day being a day we can be proud of. When we stand in a loving relationship with our own spirit and refuse to be in conflict with it, we reclaim the awe, dignity, and pride that is our birthright. When we enter into a loving relationship with our real and true self (not the artificial "positive and all smiley" one), we have many moments of valuable genuine joy. The more we go into our unhindered authenticity, the more life and love reveal themselves to us.

When we decide to uphold our unique authenticity as it is, when we say "Yes" to who we are in our true personality, we make a big leap toward standing in the ultimate "Yes"!

The Passionate "Yes" to the Sacred

The next path, the great "Yes" to the Sacred, opens us up to a willingness to dance with the Divine or the Greater Power (however we define it or name it) as a co-creative partner. We can sense that greater Presence when we allow ourselves to feel deeply and feel that we are in partnership with something greater than ourselves. There is something intensely powerful that happens when we say "Yes" to this Great Force. It leads us to a life of incredible partnership, one in which we are buttressed as well as deeply moved to help our fellow human beings and our highly stressed and struggling planet.

This great "Yes" to the Sacred is an invitation to become an authentic vessel of love and to come to realize the sacredness of love. This is amazing when we consider that we are each an expression of how the Divine shows up in the world. This great "Yes" is a willingness to step into our power as individual beings who have a calling to serve and a meaningful purpose. Saying "Yes" to the Sacred means entering into a partnership in which we recognize that we are never alone and that we have the creative force of the Universe on our side—within us and available to us! We understand that we belong to the well of love and its undying strength. This personal partnership empowers us to learn who we truly are, and how loved we are, each in our own uniqueness. How ennobling it is to know that we are loved and honored in our struggles, our failings, and in our grief. The fullness of who we are is loved and celebrated. The fullness of who we are, in our grief and joy, is appreciated and honored!

Let us not minimize the profundity of what is being suggested here. From this perspective, we are *never* alone. We are born into a relationship with the Great Other—the sacred and numinous power that brought the Universe together. We are born into this relationship—a relationship of friendship, a relationship of intense love—of being loved and loving in return. When we proclaim the passionate "Yes" to the Sacred, a deep and abiding experience of partnership becomes the foundation of our life—a close relationship no one can take away from us. It is a sense of intimate heart to Heart partnership that will allow us to move toward the ultimate "Yes."

The Passionate "Yes" to the Earth

To be aware of the importance of Planet Earth is one thing. To passionately embrace our presence on this planet is something very different. It is possible, and all too common, for people to be mere observers of this planet as though they are disconnected from it—as though the Earth is something separate from us to be coldly studied in a lab. But it is our passionate "Yes" to our Earth that helps us realize that we are an intrinsic and indivisible part of the Earth and its destiny. We are children of the Earth, made of the Earth, and we are united with the Earth in its substance. We carry its power but also its wounds. It is our passionate "Yes" to the Earth that makes us committed protectors of our environment, as well as partakers in the delights of the Earth.

However, as in any relationship, we have to say "Yes" to be able to enjoy the beauty and ecstasy of the relationship as well as fully claim our responsibility toward it. We know that the need for this "Yes," this loving commitment to our precious planet, is true. We know we can hold ourselves back and remain disconnected. But if we hold back, we do not partake in the amazing flow of beauty that our relationship with the Earth brings about! Will we continue being lulled by the lethal fantasies of systems of domination and rabid competition? Will we allow our natural environment to be destroyed by the follies of these systems? Through the passionate "Yes," we listen to the tugs and pulls of the heart. We listen for where the Earth is calling us to act. The passionate "Yes" nurtures our spirit and emboldens our strength to be present to the truth of our humanity (our earthiness) and to move forward toward the ultimate "Yes!"

> I am very fortunate that this passionate "Yes" to the Earth was passed down to me by my elders. I remember my grandmother and my great grandmother—their gardens and their love of birds. I remember my grandfather and his love of water and the trees. I remember my mother and father—my mother's love of flowers and my father's love of water and gardening. These things that have been passed down to me embody a huge appreciation for the Earth and the realization that we are both part of, as well as servants to, the Earth.
>
> I am also very fortunate to come from a legacy of individuals who have spent their lives serving the community, helping and giving back, and passing this on to the younger generations. They taught us that we are all connected and that our brothers and sisters and the Earth itself need our love and our participation. I am passing all of this on to my child and teaching her about our connection to each other and the Earth. She is learning how to care for it in the ways that she is authentically drawn—with her love of horses and dogs and her love of the sky.
>
> ~ **Mandy McMullen Bird**

Our generation is the recipient of the greatest call to action in human history. The invitation is irrevocable. The fate of the human race is at stake. What will we do with the planet of which we are entrusted stewards? Will we keep on being lulled by the lethal fantasies of systems of domination and rabid competition? Will we allow our natural environment to be destroyed by the accumulation of financial power first? Will we betray the ideals of our humanity and destroy the natural environment that sustains us? Will we betray the trust the Earth endowed us?

May we begin to think and feel on a planetary level. We are unique individuals, yet we are also indivisible from the whole of the planet. The Earth resides in us, as we reside in the Earth. May we arise to the great truth of our being. The Earth is calling us to an Olympian task of love. Act for her. Speak passionately on her behalf!

The Passionate "Yes" to the Human Struggle for Peace and Justice

The last path toward the ultimate "Yes" is through upholding and affirming the historical struggle for greater peace, greater freedom, and greater justice. This is an essential "Yes" that we need to explore, recognize, and deepen ourselves into. The struggle through many generations for greater human rights, for equality between women and men, for the end of slavery, for the establishment of greater democratic freedoms, and so on, have all shaped us and fashioned our spirits. We are the results of this great and noble struggle over thousands of years. We are like precious pieces of clay that have been molded by the hands of those grandmothers and grandfathers who courageously stood, to the best of their abilities, for a world that respects the dignity of human beings. The story of this struggle continues, and we are either part of it or we are tragically, ungratefully indifferent. There is both grief and beauty in this passionate and non-violent struggle. It is a participation in history that enlarges our heart and deepens our sense of self.

There is a great deal that needs to be done by people of heart if our human civilization is to survive. Our world today is in danger. Its future is in danger. Our democracies are besieged, and our natural environment is continuously decimated. Mega money and mega corporations are destroying the middle class. Too many people are suffering the violence of war and terrorism. To say the great "Yes" to

I want to share two more stories from part of my life—during the long and devastating war years I went through in my birthplace of Lebanon.

In my early twenties, my family owned several apartment buildings. I lived in one of them with my wife. Because of the war, we had to flee. It was a crucial moment for me when I went to visit the building during a brief ceasefire in the ongoing fighting.

Much of the building was burned. The radical group that took hold of it destroyed everything they could not steal. I decided to go to the top of the building, the elevator was not working and so I climbed the many stairs. My heart was so heavy. Our apartment was vandalized and the whole building was in very bad shape. When I reached the rooftop, I felt like my heart was going to implode. "I cannot take this," I thought. I just stood there. I was looking at the city of Beirut with lots of fire and smoke here and there, and then, all of a sudden, I felt my spirit ready to burst into singing. I actually started singing out loud and what came through me was totally unexpected. I felt that the spirit of Love is greater than any destruction, any war! Here I was, a young man in my mid-twenties, shaken and anguished, confused, grieving the loss of my home and the building where I lived, and yet there was a great song of love and strength emerging from my heart praising life and praising the Divine. That voice kept on reminding me that within me there is a power of love which is greater than any army in the world and any devastation I can experience. It is a moment I will never forget.

The other story is this: One day, during the war in Lebanon, I was driving from the mountains to my peace-making office in Beirut, and the traffic was horrible. There was a lot of shelling and people were extremely tense and edgy just wanting to reach wherever they were going as soon as possible in order to survive. Gun artillery was heavily

(Continued in next box)

pounding nearby neighborhoods. As I was waiting and wondering how long it would take to get out of this dangerous predicament, a car near me was suddenly hit by a shell and began to burn. The driver was still alive but stuck inside. Traffic stopped. Three people got out of their cars and ran to help. They were attempting to open the door to get him out. The door was jammed. I instinctually joined them.

We were all pulling at the handles, knowing that we had only minutes—if not less—to rescue him. In a flash of awareness, I realized that the car could explode at any moment, yet that did not stop any of us. Our focus was on getting that individual out of the car—the victim who, prior to that moment, was unknown to us—a stranger, as we all were to one another. I was overwhelmed by the danger of the situation but also deeply touched by the incredible beauty in the solidarity displayed. In this situation, we followed our hearts and risked our lives to reach out to a trapped and endangered fellow human being. Thankfully, we saved him before his car burst into flames. Several people volunteered to take him to the hospital and call his family.

I will never forget this experience. It was imprinted in my memory and seared into my consciousness. I will always remember that when I act from the heart, I am led to an unbounded sense of empathy and solidarity and can become the vessel for unexpected miracles. People who do not know each other can bond through an open and caring heart and even risk their lives for each other!

The well of love and care that abides in the human heart is truly astounding! Experiences like these remind us of the true human beauty and the strength that resides in the profundity of our being. We can be sarcastic as much as we want, but the truth is there, undeniable: the heart and its capacity to love generously exists and is incredibly powerful!

Afterward, back in my car on the commute, I wondered to myself, "What was that? What was that force of love that led us to do that?" I

(Continued in next box)

> was amazed at the presence of that love. I realized that my choice was to say "Yes." I had to embody and manifest, as much as possible, the beautiful energy that pulled us together to be with that guy in the car—that love which is the most delightful and powerful presence in the world. I want that in my life.
>
> **~ Chris Saade**

the non-violent struggle for a dignified life is to realize that we fully partake in the consequences of oppression or liberation. Our souls are molded by that struggle. The passion within us was brought forth by the struggle for love in order to defeat injustice and hatred. We are here to continue this crucial work, each in our authentic space of belonging. The great "Yes" to the struggle of love for greater peace, freedom, inclusion, and justice allows us to find our sense of meaning and purpose rather than succumbing to a fear that misleads us and leaves us superficially floundering. This "Yes" means that we claim our greater purpose in life; it means contributing to the evolutionary continuation of Love's great dream. Archbishop Desmond Tutu from South Africa calls it "the dream of God." We are co-creators of the great dream for peace and justice on this Earth.

This great "Yes" makes us kin to Mother Teresa and kin to Gandhi, kin to Martin Luther King Jr., and kin to all who have stood for freedom and raised their voices for solidarity. Through actively engaging in this great "Yes," we become part of causes much bigger than ourselves. Through proclaiming this great and passionate "Yes," we are called, in our own particular way, to join in solidarity with all global sisters and brothers who are making their contribution to this great "Yes." We are all part of the same movement of awakening and transformation that has gone on throughout history. Saying "Yes" to this great struggle means finding the nobility of our authentic participation within it.

One additional point is important here and needs to be made very clearly. Given the great challenges we are facing today, many of us are very concerned about the future of our humanity. When we say "Yes" to participation in the work for peace, freedom, and justice, we must do so with great passion, independent of the outcome of our efforts. We are called to show up as great "Yes"-sayers and great lovers of Planet Earth and its history.

Something that helps us say "Yes" to the struggle for peace and justice is to remember those who have struggled before us or who are struggling with us in our own lifetime. There are many powerful examples: *The Lost Boys of Sudan* were a group of young orphans who walked for as long as five years, without basic necessities and continuously in grave danger, to find safety and refuge from their war-torn country. Another example is Julia Butterfly Hill and her passionate love for saving the California Redwood forest. She is passionately engaged in the struggle to impress upon humanity how important the world's forests are for the overall health of our planet. Then there is the young Pakistani woman, Malala Yousafzai, who took such a courageous stand against the Taliban in her support of young girls' right to be educated. (In 2014, at the age of 17, she was the youngest ever recipient of the Nobel Peace Prize.) Greta Thunberg is another young woman who is fiercely and passionately calling on humanity to wake up and respond to the life-threatening climate crisis.

Remembering these inspiring examples of courageous individuals who have taken a stand for the Earth and for human values reminds us that we are part of a long and great struggle. It is important to stay connected to their lives of service and commitment; they remind us who we are in the depths of our authentic humanity. They remind us that no matter how each person is specifically called to say "Yes," each of us has a part to play in the grand story of humanity. Each of us can say a passionate "Yes" to the historical unfolding of peace and justice. We cannot assert the ultimate "Yes" if we do not also say "Yes" to the historical evolutionary struggle in which we partake, indeed because there is no way to deny our relationship to that great struggle, with all its grief and hopes.

Lessons in grief remind me of a dear friend who has done a lot of deep work around grief. One time, her daughter was in high school and experienced a very difficult failure. My friend chose to buy her daughter a gift and took her out to celebrate her effort, even though it had resulted in a great defeat. This is what it means to celebrate the fullness of our own and others' lives. If we leave our wounds and our losses out of our story and only celebrate the good times, we are not living in authenticity. It is not complete. To celebrate our defeats, as my friend did for her daughter, is to take a stand for our spirits—for our own spirit, the spirit of others we care for, and the spirit of humanity. This is to say the ultimate "Yes." It gives us the courage to go back out into the world and try again. It opens up a whole new world of bravery.

~ **Mandy McMullen Bird**

Within a short period of time in my own life, my husband at the time left me; my dearest and most cherished soul sister and business partner decided to move away; and a dear friend of mine, and of my community, went to sleep and did not wake up. These three things happened in a very short timeframe and brought me to my knees. These losses changed my work life, changed my home life, and changed my community. It was through these huge heart-breaking losses that I decided to say "Yes" to life, to keep my heart open, and to go for what I was being called to do in co-creating this grief model with Chris and manifesting a nonprofit with co-founders. I chose to say "Yes" to life as opposed to falling into despair, which would have been easy to

(Continued in next box)

do. Instead I claimed these truths and treasures within myself and am bringing them back out into the world to help others. This great "Yes" that I said, and that others have said, is reaching others and helping the world.

~ **Mandy McMullen Bird**

SECTION TWO

As we begin our exploration of the *7 Steps Toward the Power of Grief and Hope*SM, let us restate that our tears are the very source of our passion, and our passion gives us the strength and energy to do the difficult work of grieving. There is an intimate relationship between passion and grief, grief and passion. They are the two sides of the same coin—a great paradox of the life force that moves through us and motivates our being. Grief teaches us who we are and shows us what we care most about. Grief teaches us about our deepest longings and our strongest heart desires. It reveals our calling and what matters most to us in the world. Grief is to be honored as part of our true strength and not to be confused with victimization.

We, the co-authors of this book, have been teaching these ideas for many years with a desire to co-create a model that would serve as a guide—a compass to support individuals in their grief, and to ennoble and empower their grief and hope journey. What we have developed is a 7-step process. Through this model, we will guide you step-by-step through unearthing the meaning of your pain, learning to feel the full authenticity of your feelings, exploring how to mine your loss for its gifts, and allowing your grief to be the fuel for claiming a more deeply passionate and dignified life.

One of the things that has been very difficult and disempowering for most of us is the tendency to deny grief and loss. There is not much support (emotional, structural, or practical) for us to feel that it is okay to be grieving, that it is not wrong, that grief is an important part of our humanity, and to recognize that grief has its own time frame and its own pace.

This model is born out of many years of conversation and dialogue between the co-authors, in our work with individual clients, and through countless years of research and training with large groups. The model, *7 Steps Toward the Power of Grief and Hope*SM, will guide you along an empowered grief journey by giving you deeply nurturing validation and affirmation, as well as by teaching you practical tools along the way. These steps will also lead to genuine and authentic experiences of joy, helping your tears become the source of your passion.

The process outlined is not only a linear process, but also a spiral process. You can (and will most likely find that you need to) move back and forth between the steps depending on what it is you feel you need at the time. Trust yourself. That being said, there are reasons why the steps are organized the way they are. Following their order will make a lot of sense to you, but you can double-back anytime you wish.

Our hope is that you will feel supported and strengthened as you move through your grief journey. Please remember that you are not doing anything wrong by grieving or by grieving deeply—to the contrary. Also, remember that grief has its own unique timetable and way of unfolding in your life; your journey will not be the same as anyone else's. These steps will guide you in a way that will help you look for the calling in your own life and inspire you to use the wisdom you develop through your grief. Trust yourself and your own authentic process.

7 Steps Toward the Power of Grief and Hope[SM]

We developed the heart-centered model, *7 Steps Toward the Power of Grief and Hope*[SM] as a process model. While there are many models designed around the stages and transitions of grief, what makes this model special is that it is a self-coaching model, designed to support the individual through the creativity of the journey of grief. It is a model that holds the fundamental belief that the deep authenticity of the grief we feel is ultimately a treasure of life, a gift of heart and soul. The inevitable *wounds* we receive in life can become *wombs* which hold important keys to our authenticity and life calling. The steps are designed to give the individual hope as well as tools to use throughout the journey of life. In a culture that shuns grief, this model honors and upholds the dignity of grief as a necessary and powerful response to the difficult challenges we face as human beings. The steps help us to understand that developing the skills of grieving and holding hope is an integral part of our human development. This approach is designed to bring nobility and dignity to this crucial and neglected aspect of our human journey.

7 Steps Toward the Power of Grief and Hope[SM]

1. Affirm Your Grief

Honor and affirm the dignity and meaningful nature of your grief.

2. Open Your Heart

Open your heart widely. Let grief expand—not close or shrink—your heart.

3. Initiation

Mine your grief as an initiation into your deepest unique authenticity, your passionate calling, and your purpose in life.

4. Paradox

Learn to fully experience the paradoxical aspects of your authentic feelings (grief and joy). Honor both rivers of feeling that flow in you—thus experiencing the fullness of life.

5. Spiritual Fortitude

Let your own heart-spirituality be the sturdy and supportive container of your grief.

6. Service

Act. Through your grief, find your most authentic and pleasurable way of serving freedom, justice, peace, and inclusion. Then take action in the world.

7. Celebration of Life

Celebrate your *whole* life—the entirety of your authentic journey—rich in losses and blessings, failures and successes, defeats and breakthroughs.

Step One: Affirm Your Grief

Honor and affirm the dignity and meaningful nature of your grief.

Carry your wounds and grief with pride. They are a part of the greatness of your soul.

Out of our deepest wounds can arise a strength that is real, sturdy, and most generative. Do not doubt the fertile soil that exists in the profundity of your pain. From your tears, great love and passion to serve can flow. Never doubt the preciousness of your tears.

Heart-centered grief begins with honoring the meaningful nature of grief and the very important and soul-making role it has in our life. To honor our grief, we need to come to deeply respect it. Grief can feel overwhelming, as though we are being invaded against our will. However, it is crucial that we learn that our grief is a very important aspect of life and that it will, in the end, bestow us with great blessings. Grief can be devastating if not approached intentionally and skillfully. However, skilled grieving can also unleash our passionate creativity and allow our heart to feel more deeply, to feel more love for others, and to feel more love for the world and the Earth. Our deep grief can open the doors of empathy toward people of heart—including compassion for our own individual self. Honoring grief is honoring the depth and richness of our human nature. We honor our grief to dignify it—to view it not as something unworthy or horrible but rather as something (no matter how challenging) that flows from the deep truth and sensitivity of our loving heart. When we befriend our grief, we find our way through. In this section we will delve more deeply into the idea of honoring our grief, which we initially touched-on in Section One, as well as explore some practical tools for affirming grief.

One of the important questions people have raised about grief is its relation to victimization. Nobody wants to feel like a victim, but does deeply feeling our grief inherently make us a victim? The answer is an absolute "No." One of the most tragic disservices to humanity is the fact that we have been taught to see our grief as something that victimizes us. "I do not want to feel like a victim!" is a common refrain. But when we view our grief from this misguided perspective, we miss the deep truth that we are being given a treasure and an insight into life and who we really are. Grieving well is part of our strength. Victimization is a weakening attitude and orientation that has nothing to do with grief or the lack thereof. We know that when something tragic and heart-wrenching happens in people's lives, something powerful within us begins to surface. We know this from our own personal experience and from witnessing family members, friends, colleagues, and historical figures who we look up to and admire. But if we perceive grief as victimizing, this powerful and life-giving emergence is blocked. We can and need to grieve without feeling victimized. We can grieve with honor and dignity. We can grieve while standing in our power and refuse to think of ourselves as helpless victims.

We have been taught that our grief makes us feel crazy. It is almost seen as a pathology—as though something is very wrong with us—when in truth something very human, very valuable, and very sacred is occurring. Whatever our loss is, however profoundly it breaks our heart, something noble and dignified is happening when we bravely engage our wounds. We can think of our grief as an "angel" that mirrors back to us the depth of who we really are and what our gifts are. The great travesty is that we have been shown the treasure of our heart intelligence, yet we are taught to feel ashamed and told to shake it off and get over it. We may have been taught that if we are hurting deeply, we are not strong or tough enough, when in actuality, our broken heart reflects the fullness of our being and our true strength. We must learn to trust, honor, and respect this process.

We must learn that our grief is our friend because when something sad and heart-breaking happens, the masks we often wear fall off and we can no longer overlook our true authenticity. If we numb our feelings or medicate them through abuse of alcohol or drugs to avoid grief, we ironically become weaker, more artificial, often depressed and very vulnerable to thoughts of victimization.

Opening up your heart and choosing to encounter and excavate your grief means that you welcome it and honor it as a great source of wisdom. Let your grief be your friend. Stop ignoring, pretending, numbing, and minimizing this powerful life force. Seek the wisdom that the authenticity of your grief wants to teach you about your self and about your spirit.

Thus, the first and most fundamental questions to ask ourselves are: "Do we view our grief as a victimizing enemy? Or do we view our grief as an honorable and essential experience that helps us learn who we really are and what our calling is?" If we perceive grief as victimization, we pollute and derail the natural and life-giving grieving process. We go into despair and isolate ourselves from the people around us, including those who want to help because they are facing similar struggles and pain.

We can choose to grieve without victimization. Falling into a victim mentality makes it harder for us to grasp the sacred and dignified nature of our grief. Our task is to grieve without falling into the fallacy of victimization—to grieve without losing our sense of individual power and refusing to separate our sense of power from our grieving.

When shaming voices assail you saying that you have been sad for too long, it is essential that you push back and say a radical "No!" It is important to grieve for as long as you feel the need to grieve. Do not fight your grief. Refuse any thoughts of yourself as impotent or victimized.

One practical thing that helps is to have meaningful visual symbols in your home that remind you of the essential grace and power of your grief. Think about what drawing, painting, sculpture, or photograph you can put in your home that symbolizes the dignity of grief. What artwork can you put in your home to comfort you, encourage you, and inspire you to honor your grief and allow it to be your companion? Our sacred grief is a companion that always unfolds and leads us to deeper and deeper knowing of our passion and sense of meaning and joy.

You are not alone in your grief. You are not alone because there is suffering throughout the world; every other human being on the planet shares in the experience of grief. There is an epidemic of divorces and dead relationships. There is poverty. There are wars. There are economic problems. There is unemployment. There are illnesses and death. We each have a share in the suffering of the world because we are part of the world and we are the world. You are not alone because you are one with the world. And you are not alone because the Source of Life—in any way you name it—is with you. You are never alone when you walk consciously and proudly through your suffering. In addition, the ancestors who have suffered are with you in your conscious and subconscious memory. They and the ancients before them have walked, struggled, suffered, and emerged stronger again and again throughout humanity's long history. This is part of the human story and part of the life journey in which we all share.

We are part of a continuum of the past, the present, and the future of humanity. We are striving to be fully human and to do our part to help evolve consciousness. Recognizing that we are not alone, but rather one with the tears of the world, is essential in befriending our grief and affirming its dignified importance. If we remind ourselves on a daily basis, with our symbols around us, that we are not alone and that we are part of the matrix of life, then our grief opens us up to a communion with the world's suffering. We are in touch with other people's suffering and, if you are a believer, with the pain held in the heart of the Divine herself who is grieving all oppression and pain in the world. Our suffering opens us up to a deeper understanding of our place in the Universe. Thus, we come to seriously honor our tears and our sadness. We come to honor this humanizing unfolding.

Having images around you that remind you of the dignity of grief can include making use of your computer. Go to the internet and search for images of grief and suffering. You will find countless works reflecting the universality and dignity of suffering. Find images of people you respect—like Mother Teresa, Gandhi, Martin Luther King Jr., or Florence Nightingale. You will realize that they also experienced immense suffering and they carried that grief, but they learned to carry it with nobility and pride, and they definitely mined its creativity. These are images that mirror back to us the power of the grief process and its honorability.

We may ask ourselves why if feels so bad when we feel our grief. We are tempted to get busy and do something else to forget about all the sadness and heaviness we are carrying in our heart and body. We are afraid it will lead us to depression. Of course, depression is something that everyone wants to (and should fight to) avoid. There is this fear that if we feel our grief, it will turn into a bottomless depression. We might weep and weep and fear that we will never again be able to do anything useful in our life or for the lives of others. We fear we will permanently lose our ability to be able to do our jobs, feed our children, or perform our roles in society! But scientifically and clinically this is not true. It is *not*.

This is a crucial understanding. It is when we reject our grief that sadness becomes very painful. When we welcome our grief, the nature of our grief becomes life-giving. When grief knocks on your door and you keep the door closed, it will knock harder and louder. When you open the door and invite your grief in, the relationship eases and gradually becomes a life-giving and creative partnership. So it is when we welcome our grief.

It is our responsibility to protect ourselves from depression. Those who love us need our spirit to be alive and passionate. The Earth needs our spirit to be alive and passionate.

There are two different essential forms of depression: clinical depression and depression-of-the-spirit. It is possible to experience both forms simultaneously which makes it very important to be aware of each form and the different ways to address each. *Neither of these debilitating conditions is caused by grief.*

Let us examine the differences more closely. Clinical depression envelops us in a paralyzing abyss. It deprives us of the ability to experience the paradoxes of life: grief and joy, anger and peace, anxiety and excitement. We become stuck, emotionally paralyzed, and totally drained. This could be at a cognitive level or at an emotional level, and there are chemical and physical aspects to it. For this reason, clinical depression calls for the professional services of a psychotherapist, psychiatrist, or both to help address the clinical aspects of what is going on.

When we go through a depression-of-the-spirit, we lose our motivation. It is not a clinical depression, yet we find it very difficult to access our passion. We are uninspired. We feel that nothing matters very much. It could be in the domain of relationship, work, or social activism. We feel drained, emptied, and passive. We are not in the deep abyss of clinical depression, however almost nothing is enlivening our heart. Very little fills us with energy and excitement. When we *avoid* grieving, we experience this type of depression. This is the price we pay for numbing our feelings and living in denial. Our sense of vision is lost. Our sense of power and strength is lost. And when pushed to the extreme, depression-of-the-spirit can develop into a clinical depression. Depression-of-the-spirit is a much more common ailment than clinical depression. Depression-of-the-spirit calls for the awakening of passion. Discovering and unlocking our passion is crucial and can help break this form of depression's draining hold on us. Grief, when approached intentionally and skillfully using a heart-centered approach, will birth a passionate desire or calling that will lead us out of a depression-of-the-spirit.

> If your grief is strong, it would be a great help to reach out to grief-support groups in your community and online. We also strongly recommend doing personal therapy—with the caveat that the therapist you choose has done his or her own grief and authenticity journey. It is essential that you choose a group and/or a therapist that can be with you in the intensity of your grief and honor the depths of your pain. As you reach out for support and embrace your grief journey, you will learn more and more about yourself. But wherever you go for support, make very sure you find places that respect your grief as part of the honored journey of life. If you hear anyone speaking about grief as a pathology, a sickness, or as something negative to avoid and extricate from your life, then stay away. Always go to people who can sincerely honor your grief. This is extremely important to remember.
>
> **~ Mandy McMullen Bird**

So, to reiterate, grief does not *cause* depression. It is the *denial and numbing of grief* which increase any kind of depression. Our spirit thrives by being authentic; and being authentic means that we feel the sadness visiting us, and we feel the joy that is there too. We experience all of our feelings and refuse to deny their profundity. When we allow any part of our feelings, particularly our sadness or anguish to be shamed or to be seen as inappropriate, wrong, or something to avoid at any cost, then a paralysis develops in the psyche. Therefore, it is so important to recognize that our strength comes from our authenticity. Authenticity is the foundation of our power.

Living with depression-of-the-spirit is very difficult for any human being; it is essential to be wary of and alert to its dangers. We must push back against the cultural messages that tell us not to feel deeply, not to experience our grief, and not to take time to nurture the depth of our pain. The destructive voices that tell us to hurry up and get on with it need to be rejected. These misguided pressures do not allow us to be fully human and deprive us from the wisdom of grief—both individually and collectively.

How needed it is today, on a global scale, for us to feel the grief of the destructive forces attempting to deconstruct democracy and replace it with authoritarian and nationalistic regimes! This requires, quite simply, a rebellion of the heart—a rejection of the cultural message that says you will feel better if you avoid grieving when something sad or tragic happens, as if grief is a plague! What really helps is the willingness and courage to actually experience those feelings to their depths. This is what protects us from depression-of-the-spirit. This is what births within us visions of love and action!

Another essential point is that when you experience your grief intentionally and in a heart-centered manner, your grief will integrate into your life in a way that is healthy and empowering. It is like color in a painting. Great paintings are not only made from bright, joyful colors, they also include deep blacks, browns, and grays. It is when all of the colors are integrated that the painting takes on a greater dimension of beauty and power. It is the same thing in life. "Intentional" means you choose—you choose to let your grief occupy an honored place in your heart. This might seem like a lot to ask, but by being conscious every day about how you relate to your grief—and by choosing to accept and honor your human destiny of joy *and* grief, blessings *and* losses—you are empowered by the energy of life itself. You become at peace with the paradoxes of life and with your own life. You stop fighting the reality of your precious humanity. You also realize that your grief is a shared experience with the struggle of others. It is a participation with the suffering of the world that allows you to honor your grief as a communion with the world. Instead of: "Why me? Why am I suffering? Why am I challenged? Why am I sad? What is wrong with me?"—you come to realize that your grief is a participation with everyone in the world who knows oppression, who knows poverty, who knows illness, who knows loss and suffering, and who knows rejection. You come to honor the collective profound meaning of your grief.

When we develop an intentional and conscious relationship with grief, we become more human, more empathic, and more part of the human and animal community.

Another question we often hear is: "Why is my grief so intense and why is it taking so long for me to move through this process?" It is tempting to try to speed up the process or to try to control it. We think to ourselves, "Yes, I will begin going to therapy or will participate in a support group, but I had better be done quickly." This is a common position. But the reality is that, whether we like it or not, the grieving process is a great mystery. It depends on the situation and the individual. Grief has a life of its own which must be respected. There is no time limit for grief. We must make room for it in our life without judgment and with great respect and honor for the time and forms it takes. We need to remember that significant wounds never go away. Over time our wounds become less raw and slowly evolve and grow into rich additions to the tapestry of our lives. The patience required is not easy because we live in a busy, fast-paced culture in which time is money, speed is valued, and we all feel that pressure every single day. We are also bombarded with the injunction to "be positive" rather than to feel *human* and *authentic*. The grieving journey unfolds at a human pace and in a manner that is unique to your authenticity. This is the time in your life in which you must learn to trust that unfolding.

So often we fight the process. We think we should be able to press a button, and something will instantly happen. But of course, that is not the way it is with the grieving process and the human heart. In the depth of your own wisdom, you know that you must respect the time and the space that it takes for grief to settle in you and reveal its gold to you. The heart has its own time.

As you affirm and honor your grief, do your best in your internal conversation to say, "I know I do not get to pick how long it is going to take. I need to allow this grieving process to naturally unfold and to trust that my authentic way of grieving will empower me into a deeper knowing of my own spirit and strength." This requires patience and trusting in the power of your own authenticity.

The good news is, the less you try to control your grief and the more you befriend it, the more its pain will abate. The grief will have its own process, but the debilitating and paralyzing pain will start to diminish as you let it find its own way through.

It is important here to address the anger that is a natural part of the grief process. Anger should not be used to replace sorrow. But anger has its rightful place alongside sorrow. Anger is an emotion which, like all emotions, when expressed or held unconsciously and unintentionally, can be used destructively and become dangerous for ourselves and others. However, conscious anger and outrage can bequeath us and others with a multitude of gifts if handled intentionally and with maturity.

Anger is destructive when we carelessly lash out at ourselves or at others. Blind and impulsive anger becomes untethered rage. It becomes an out-of-control emotion that hurts us and others and can cause real damage. The purpose of intentional anger stemming from your grief is to call you into a period of fierce discernment and honest self-reflection. It raises the questions: "What boundaries are absolutely necessary for me? What aspects of my authenticity have I betrayed and need to faithfully restore? Who are the people I am allowing to drain me or hurt my spirit? Where am I acting out of guilt or an imposed sense of responsibility? And where do I need to claim the freedom to invest my love where my heart desires?" and so forth… Or on a broader cultural level: "What oppression or injustice am I called to stand against? What intentional words or actions is my anger spurring me to express in the name of liberation and love?"

Let us reiterate that, contrary to many "positive" and spiritual ideologies, anger is a very important and normal part of grief and a great generator of insight and wisdom. But it must not be blindly acted out. Anger is an invitation for a thorough house cleaning. We are asked to act on anger's insights with grace, nobility, and committed non-violence. If you are not able to do so, it means you have not finished your inner reflection. Do not lash out with your anger; instead use its power to fuel your inner exploration, your respectful inquisitive dialogue with others, or your courageous sacred activism.

It is also very important to protect yourself from the belief that somehow, if you take certain "magical" steps, you will get rid of your grief (with its natural sorrow, anguish, and anger) and everything will be okay. There are people who teach this formulaic approach; the problem is that it makes you feel even worse about yourself because you will realize that your grief is still there. (Remember we are all wounded, and we learn to thrive as wounded people.) So, in addition to the original grief, you feel as though you have failed because you could not get rid of your grief. This creates more suffering on top of the grief you are already experiencing. You might start asking: "What is so wrong with me that I cannot get over my grief?" Then you start a perpetual cycle of feeling even worse about your own spirit. The purpose of this work is to befriend your grief and learn tools and concepts that can support and empower you as you move through the paralyzing acuity of the pain. When this is achieved, your grief—

along with your joy—will be integrated as a component of your beautiful humanity. You will also be able to feel the ecstasy of love and a sense of being at peace with yourself. Invite and honor the depth of your grief and do not question its presence nor its intensity. Never shame yourself for your intensity. Also, stay graceful, do not replace your tears with aggression; respect the intensity of anger that can accompany your sorrow. Your grief is a measure of your humanity. It is something to welcome with honor and dignity—no matter how deep your river of grief is. There are tools to help you in that process, for example, the critical tool of holding paradox. We will discuss these in the upcoming steps.

Here are a few simple tools you can use. First, write a few sentences about the sacred or dignified nature of your grief on a card, or on several cards, and keep them where you can read them throughout your day. Second, re-read this section whenever shame or helplessness about your grief surface. Our society does not nurture us in our grief, so it is critical to nurture yourself deeply and intensely with pleasure and sustenance—this will create a protective and strengthening balm to help you hold and engage the sharp edges of your grief. Remind yourself over and over that, ultimately, your grief is a life-giving force that can open and deepen your heart and expand your ability to love—to love your authentic spirit, to love those you respect and hold dear, and to also love the beauty of the Earth and the world. Practice honoring and upholding the dignity and sacred beauty of your sadness.

> As I shared previously, I am a survivor of emotional child abuse and that has left me with an immense level of grief. I also witnessed the devastation of my country during the war in Lebanon. During my participation in the peace movement, I saw Beirut, a city that I love, burn twice. I lost everything during that war and my family lost everything
>
> (Continued in next box)

too. We ended up as exiles. This was throughout my 20s and my 30s, and I was left with an immense amount of sorrow. It broke my heart.

For a long time, I felt that this grief was denying me life; it felt like I had lost my chance for life because I was carrying so much grief. I thought that I was handed the "bad card" in some great cosmic game—until, through a lot of self-development and learning, I was able to see that I was not missing out on life, that grief is part of life, and that grief is part of my life. I came to see my grief was a sacred and authentic aspect of my life that helped transform me, open my heart, enriched me, and is part of what makes me the person I am. I realized that feeling my grief makes more room in my heart for grief's twin of joy. I realized that I must honor that grief and welcome it as very important in my life. Those realizations shifted my relationship to grief. I started to honor my grief, to see it as a sacred part of my life experience.

Regarding my childhood emotional abuse, I initially struggled with the great sadness generated by the memories of those long lasting very difficult years of my youth. I tried to do everything to forget those years and to forget about my deep sadness. I would even read literature that encouraged me to forget my past. Such teachers of positive thinking would say: "Put it behind you. Put it behind you. Put it behind you." But that approach weakened me and brought me many severe anxiety attacks. It was only when I learned to embrace my grief and say to myself: "No, this is not a curse. This is part of my life. This is part of my destiny. Let me face it. Let me respect it. Let me embrace it and mine its gifts." Only then could I start to emerge with strength and pride about who I was and the truth of my story.

I also felt like I was carrying a lot of the burdens of suffering that most people did not. Others seemed to smile continuously. They were all doing "fine and well." I felt alone and isolated, and this added to my

(Continued in next box)

sense of being alone with my pain. It was only when I realized that suffering is part of the destiny of every human being, however thoroughly many deny it, that my thinking started to shift. As I began to understand that suffering is a part of the evolutionary journey itself and that I had the power to claim and mine life-giving gifts out of my pain, my loneliness and isolation were replaced with spiritual awareness and a sense of being at deep peace with myself.

~ Chris Saade

Step Two: Open Your Heart

Open your heart widely. Let grief expand—not close or shrink—your heart.

Keep your heart open no matter what. It is your heart that is the altar of your love and your true strength.

Step two is about opening your heart to your grief and allowing it to move through you and expand your heart in the process. It is essential to reiterate here what we made clear in the introduction: Grief (in all its forms and feelings of heartbreak, heaviness, anguish, or anger) is our natural and intelligent response to being wounded. Opening our heart to and befriending our grief is about honoring this powerful response. This is *not* about befriending the *causes* of our wounding, especially the wounds from abuse or oppression. What we are advocating is an opening to the deep authentic truth of our own being and experiences while also clearly and fiercely opposing abuse and oppression in our own lives and in the world.

As you learn to befriend the authenticity of your grief, your heart will become a larger container for all of your feelings. Shutting down, numbing, or denying your heart only damages you emotionally and physically. (Remember that shutting down our heart should not be confused with the very important and protective skills of maintaining healthy boundaries and intentional avoidance of toxic people or situations.) The more you open your heart to the depth of your grief, the more life and all its marvels will dwell in it. What will help you and inspire you is to open your heart more and more every day in order to create a larger space to house your deep grief and all your deep feelings.

The common temptation, when we have experienced an event that has wounded us, is to close our heart, shut down, pull in, and be on guard. Many people, when they have been deeply hurt by life, say to themselves, "I am not going to open my heart again. I will not take that chance again." We have all thought this—and felt it. But times of wounding are, in fact, times in life when it is *essential* to open your heart, again, not to *what* or *who* wounded you, but to the powerful and natural response of your own authentic being. Allowing your heart to get bigger and fuller enables your grief to do its work. It means you let yourself feel and go deeper into the intelligence of your feelings. Engaging your grief is one of the powerful pathways to learning from your mistakes and gaining insight about your authentic self, others, and the realities of the world. If you close off your heart, if you withdraw and say, "I am not going to take a risk again. I am not going to let anyone close to me again. I am not going to engage and pursue my dreams and passions," then you miss out on your destiny and what life is co-creating with you.

This step is about opening, trusting, and allowing your heart to expand and widen so you can go into a deeper experience of life and love. You will recognize that regardless of the pain you are in, the things you want for your life cannot come to you if you close your heart. This is the time to gather up your courage, no matter how deeply wounded you are, and make a conscious decision to keep your heart awake, open, and alive. As time goes by, you will discover a deeper wisdom arising in you. You will begin to feel a deeper sense of connection to all humanity. It takes time and trust to open up, but making this choice is something you will never regret. It is a choice you make from the depths of your suffering—a choice to be open to life so you can be guided to a much deeper empathy and a greater sense of calling.

A common question we hear from people who have been struggling through a time of grief is: "My heart is being shattered; what should I do?" When you are going through great loss, when you are experiencing breakdowns and great disappointments, you will feel like your whole heart is breaking into pieces. We have been taught to believe that shutting down our heart is an effective way to protect ourselves. But what is essential to remember is that while our heart-shattering causes pain, the most intense pain comes from trying to avoid the reality of our authentic response to the difficulties and brutality of life. Unfortunately, we have learned to distrust and repress our powerful authentic responses to life. We are taught not to let others, or the world, touch us profoundly. Yet we, as intelligent and sensitive human beings, are created and meant to feel deeply. The deep rivers of feeling flowing through us are an incredible strength and one we must cultivate and channel with wisdom and intentionality. In an experience of deep grief, these stifling defenses can be replaced with our conscious grieving. If we allow it to, this intentional vulnerability humanizes us, sculpts our spirit, and expands our ability to love and be passionate.

It is so important to remember that our greatest wealth in life is our authentic heart. It is this heart that allows us to love our partners, our children, our friends, the world, and the Earth itself. It is this open heart that allows us to love what is sacred and to be awed by the Universe. There is nothing that compares to an authentic heart. We all know that some people can acquire a great deal in life but if their heart is still somehow closed, they miss out on all that is worthy. Our authentic heart is our greatest wealth.

Once we commit to open our heart, we come to understand more about what is happening within the process of grief. Our undammed and conscious grieving shatters the prison of superficiality and inauthentic facades obscuring the truth of our heart. Our empowered grief blazes a path of greater depth of feeling and passion. When we feel more deeply, we begin to feel everything. We sense beauty more intensely. We acquire greater potential to feel happiness and even ecstasy. The ideals that guide our life become clearer. But we will also feel sorrow because it is the same heart that feels all feelings across the spectrum. What we call the "breaking of the heart" is really the expanding ability of the heart to feel more deeply about our loss, and thus, about life and all of our experiences.

It is all too easy to think if we experience feelings strongly in life, then it means a life of pain. Pain and pleasure are part of life and are powers within life. If we close our heart and refuse to feel, then the repressed pain not only blinds our vision but also festers and gets worse. If we commit to keep our heart open to feelings and to love through the storm, then we learn to integrate pain and make it part of the canvas of who we are; we develop the skills to discover the rich gifts from the well of our wounds. As we open our heart to consciously integrate the pain we are facing, that pain becomes much less acute. Our task is to learn to navigate pain while mining its gifts and its treasures of wisdom. We achieve this through an open heart which refuses to turn bitter and shut down. We have to remember that the whole world is hurting and so are we. There are amazing breakthroughs, inventions, and achievements to celebrate in the world, but there is also a lot of pain. There are about 500 million children who are undernourished and suffering. There are too many countries experiencing wars and civil strife. There is racial tension. There is abuse of women and disregard for women's dignity. Feeling the truth is an essential part of growth, strength, and wisdom. If we refuse to allow the heart to feel and integrate pain, then we will be unable to feel great joy and love. The heart is one, and it holds it all.

When your heart stays open no matter what, it begins to free you from isolation and enables you to develop a sense of a larger global participation. The belief in individualistic isolation is a prison. Many people are rabid socialites, yet feel very cut off from others, from a sense of meaning, and from the world at large. They get imprisoned by thinking (and believing) that their socializing is the beginning and the end of it all. This is stifling. It makes our personal issues so big and so heavy to carry. But when the heart is visited by grief and starts breaking, it is this breaking that becomes the opening for the world to enter. Calling begins to take precedence over superficiality and vanity, thereby allowing love to deliver to us our deepest sense of authenticity and our highest calling. An open and feeling heart can hear its calling and generate the passion needed to pursue that calling and walk its destiny.

Becoming aware of our own defenses is a most useful tool. Pay attention and ask yourself some questions: "Am I isolating myself? Do I guard my heart from those who truly love me? Do I keep myself from being deeply moved, impacted, or touched by the people near me? Am I indifferent to the lyrics of a song that once moved me or numb to artwork that once held meaning for me? Am I guarding myself from life and love? Am I afraid to feel?"

Pay attention to your internal conversation. How are you talking to yourself about your hurting, grieving heart? Are you shaming yourself? Are you saying things like: "Come on, just get over it. Pull yourself up by your bootstraps. Just move on and shut off your feelings"? Or are you listening to your heart and respecting it? Learn this distinction. Pay attention to the ways you unintentionally block your heart. Learn to recognize these self-defeating injunctions so you can make different choices. Take the time to journal and write down three ways in which you fence off your heart. Without self-judgement, write down the ways in which you are defending yourself against your loss, your broken heart, your grief. Identifying your responses will help you immensely in becoming conscious, intentional, and aware of what you are doing. When you decide to honor your grief and courageously keep your heart open, you become your own best ally.

Another fear that frequently arises is that our broken heart will paralyze us. This leads to a powerful question we are well served to ask ourselves: “How can I function in the world and in my life with a broken heart?” This is a question we, the authors, have personally explored ourselves, and also explored with many, many clients. How do we move passionately through our life and through the world while at the same time feeling extremely brokenhearted? The answer rests in our ability to receive the rich gifts of grief. A conscious broken heart can discover the powerful gifts of empathy for others and gentleness toward our self. Our skilled grieving matures our love and seeds us with wisdom in our relationship with the world. Our broken heart holds power, not weakness. We are in a world that is hurting and needs our seasoned and authentic leadership. Our broken-open heart is a gift to the world. This is not merely a poetic assertion; it is reality! By allowing ourselves to move through the world and attend to our responsibilities with both a wounded heart and an equally joyful and strong heart, we will be more genuine, more empathic, and more creative, as well as more passionate and intelligent. We will be better parents, better romantic partners, better workers, and better managers. The artificiality that results from shutting and hiding the truth of our heart actually diminishes our creativity immensely and seriously clouds our minds. Authenticity is the source of love, power, and true efficiency.

It is a practical reality that the more you keep your heart open, the more you will develop empathy for other good-hearted human beings and discover the passion to love the people and tasks you are called to love. When people become unable to know the depth of love, when they stop caring about the world and only care about their own survival, it is because they have closed off their heart and shut themselves down.

They implode into their own suffering and are focused only on their personal loss. This creates even more pain and suffering for themselves and our world.

Consider this, the greatest of heroes are wounded heroes. The greatest leaders are wounded leaders. The greatest mothers and fathers are wounded mothers and fathers. To be able to function in the world with a heart that is hurting, we must remember that the wounded heart is part of our reality as human beings and spiritual creatures. Our wound does not stop us from functioning; rather, it empowers us and deepens our wisdom so we can act in a transformative way in this hurting world. Our wounds, when intentionally integrated and honored, will humanize us and greatly deepen our wisdom.

The rejection of the wounded heart is a tyranny imposed on the authenticity of our spirit. Such a rejection imposes on us a false positive image of self as though we are meant to always be happy, peaceful, and doing great every moment of every day! We need to understand the stultifying danger of this falsehood, and thus, work to overcome it.

Another critical step is to ask friends whom you trust for their support and blessing. To begin, avoid isolating yourself. As you grieve and as the tears flow and the sadness surfaces, recognize your feelings and then resist running away. Make requests for support and blessings; asking for blessings as you grieve is a gift to those close to you as well as to yourself. Avoid asking or allowing others to help you fix or heal your grief—for one thing, this is not possible, and for another, it thwarts your ability to mine your grief for its gifts and wisdom. Instead, ask for kindness, understanding, and a respectful honoring of your courageous grieving.

Blessing is an incredible and powerful tool. And *you* hold the power of blessing your broken heart. As you do so, your heart opens even more. By knowing the power of blessing your grief, you will also know that you can function in the world as a full human being—with sadness as well as with joy.

This brings us to a spiritual question that many people ask. But before we address this question, we first want to repeat this, because it is essential to make this very clear: *when we speak about spirituality, we speak about it with respect for all different faiths, beliefs, and philosophies that honor love and human dignity in this world.* The question is: "When I pray and pray, and ask to be freed from my grief, and do not feel any relief, why is God not answering?" The same question could be worded as: "Why is Life not answering?" When we are on our knees in grief and despair, why does it so often feel that we are abandoned? This is a critical question as is the answer.

For those who believe in a divine source or a higher power, let us remember that the Divine accompanies us in our human journey; strengthens us; fills us with love and nurturing; supports us; holds our hand; walks in front of us, next to us, and behind us. But the Divine cannot change the essential reality of life. We are living in a paradoxical reality of joy and struggle, blessings and losses, breakthroughs and defeats. It is an evolving reality within us and within the world.

The world is still struggling toward greater peace, justice, compassion, solidarity, and inclusion. But it is a slow process of evolution which happens through setbacks, difficulties, and challenges. It is the same for us as individuals. We are evolving and learning how to be one with the world through these challenges. Those who love greatly despite it all, those who give generously from the wellspring of their authenticity, they have learned to accept the full and paradoxical reality of their humanity. Their prayer is answered in that they are given the strength and support to keep their heart open—to keep on loving and pursuing their passion, *through* their tears and their human anguish.

When we accept the reality of life and the sacredness of our grief, God or Life will fill us with strength, presence, and nurturance. Our time spent moving through grief is sacred in the sense that it is fertile with the discovery of one's self and of one's calling. With the courage to face reality in its fullness, we stand on holy ground.

If we are people of faith or spirituality, it is very important to realize that the Divine is with us, not to rid us of our grief, but to help strengthen us as we learn to walk through our grief and integrate it with pride. As we embrace our grief, we become more human, stronger, and more compassionate; we come to love justice more; to love freedom, peace, and inclusion more; and to be more in solidarity with what is noble in the world. God is with us in that transformative growth process. This is the faith of sacred companionship.

> During my experiences working in areas of wrenching poverty and in places suffering from war, I have witnessed that God was never closer than when communing with people who were wounded, struggling, or broken-hearted. In the space of grief and suffering, when we invite in the sacred Presence, we truly stand on holy ground.
>
> **~ Chris Saade**

You can incorporate a practice into your everyday routine that will allow you to feel connected to the Source of life. When you are deeply wounded and grieving, it is too easy to feel separated from life itself or the Divine. The practice is to create a daily time and a space for yourself that allows you to be in silence and to carefully listen to your own heart. It could be a time of prayer, a quiet walk in nature, a time of meditation, a moment where you can stop the busyness and be fully in your own body. You will come to feel your heart, know your own mind, and sense your spirit. What are your heart, your own true thoughts, and your spirit saying to you? Remember, do not ask for your grief to magically disappear. Rather, listen to what your grief is attempting to tell you. Keep your heart wide open and seek the significant gifts of insight and vision from your well of grief. They will come to you.

To summarize, we have covered three essential questions: "My heart feels like it is shattering; what do I do?" The answer is to understand the process of shattering. Our heartbreak over the wounds and suffering we endure, so much of which is unavoidable, is a manifestation of our natural intelligence and our deep capacity to love and care passionately. We must learn to stand proudly in our woundedness honoring our courage and strength to live and love fully in the face of great challenges. Understand heartbreak as the chrysalis that is breaking so the butterfly can emerge and fly free. Let your heart break so it can enter into a great and loving empathy with the world.

The second question is: “I am afraid that if I let my heart be broken, I will be paralyzed. How will I be able to function in the world?” We all are called to function in the world with our broken heart. We are all called to walk heartfully as wounded healers; as wounded leaders; as wounded parents; as wounded friends, partners, and spouses. In our woundedness we walk knowing joy, knowing love, and knowing the wounded world—within and without. This means entering into a loving, respectful, and dignified relationship with our grief.

Question three is a deep spiritual question: “Why is God not ridding me of my grief when I pray and pray?” When we pray, we do not pray for magic. We pray for the companionship of the Divine. If we ask the Divine to take away our grief, it means we are asking to have our humanity taken away. Instead, we ask the Divine to walk with us, to be our companion, to support us, and to help us embrace our heart and our humanity even more fully. We pray for God to walk with us, for the energy of Life to strengthen us, for the Divine to walk with us *through it all*. Remember that the grief in your life is a treasure that cannot be mined if your heart is not open. When we are deeply hurting and feeling the temptation to close off and shut down, we must remember that this is the very time we must keep our heart open, awake, and alive. This will allow our grief to grow into a gentle experience in which greater love can emerge as we come to fulfill our calling.

It is essential to understand the place of the heart in the human journey and in the evolution of humankind. As human beings, we are coming to realize that if we are to solve the problems threatening our planet and humanity, we need a heightened intelligence that comes only from the passion and the compassion of an open and loving heart. The mind, while essential, is not enough by itself. It is the heart setting a direction for the mind that will bring us to be fully engaged, to be active, to connect with people from different traditions, and to envision significantly better possibilities for our planet.

This is where evolution is leading us: to thoroughly develop and open the fullness of our feeling heart. Once we understand this in its global and universal significance, we will better understand and accept what is happening to us personally. We will see that our authentic, empowered, and creative response to the pain of life, as well as its joy, is vital for developing the strong heart that engages us in life and enables us to become passionate visionaries and leaders in the transformation and peace-building of the world itself.

I have had many losses in my life. I really know what it is like to be dropped to your knees. It can feel so shocking and so surprising. During those times, even with all the work I have done and my expertise, I have moments of thinking to myself "How in the world am I going to go on? How am I going to get up in the morning? How am I going to take care of myself and take care of my daughter and tend to my practice? How will I stay engaged in my life and my relationships, go to the grocery store, do my laundry, make my bed? How can I keep functioning on a practical level every single day with a broken heart?" Whenever I have experienced this type of loss, it has been very important that I continually reach out for support. For me, this means reaching out to friends, to therapists, to coaches, and calling on my relationship with the Divine. I read all types of scripture, books, and encouraging poetry—any type of material that helps me stay in my power and in my heart. I always make a huge effort to resist numbing

(Continued in next box)

out in any way. I work hard to stay engaged with my heart, and I do this by talking to myself, staying in contact with my self through journaling, and paying attention to my inner dialogue and how I speak to myself.

For example, when my marriage ended, I felt completely shattered and asked myself everything mentioned above··· I did not know how I was going to keep moving forward. What I discovered is that to truly live the life that I want to live, I have to stay engaged. I have to stay connected to my self and the world no matter how devastating the loss and pain.

~ Mandy McMullen Bird

I want to address my own belief system in a God that is love. So often in the past, I have been on my knees praying and praying, "God, free me from my grief. Free me from my grief. Free me from my difficult memories of pain. Let it be behind me. Let me move forward." But I realized that God was not answering these prayers in the way I wanted. God was not transforming my life into a panacea. I discovered that God was walking alongside me, holding my hand as I walked through the truth and the reality of the world and of my grief. I have experienced wounding and pain at many crossroads in my life. I realized that there is no force that frees us from the challenges of the world. This is why it is so dangerous to our heart, our dignity, and our well-being to hear others blaming us along the lines of, "You are responsible for your own disease," or "You have created your own tragedy." Tragedy is part of life. The relevant question is "Do we build islands of beauty and celebration in our troubled circumstances?"

I think about Mary, the mother of Jesus. She took great joy and pride in being able to walk alongside Jesus and to witness all that was happening throughout his ministry. But what tremendous grief she also

(Continued in next box)

carried in her heart from the persecution her son endured and, ultimately, his experience on the cross itself. Mary is a beautiful example of a woman who walked life with a loving and nurturing heart—a heart that could feel joy but also a heart that was wounded. We must free ourselves from ideas that say we should not be wounded and that there is something wrong with us if we are. I had to learn to be proud and worthy of my wounds. My task is to keep my heart open, to hold each of my wounds with authenticity and strength, and to work to discover their many creative gifts.

~ Chris Saade

Step Three: Initiation

Mine your grief as an initiation into your deepest unique authenticity, your passionate calling, and your purpose in life.

There are times in our life when loss feels as though it cannot be survived. Life as we know it collapses, and we go through a very dark time—so dark that we wonder if we will be able to emerge from it. It can be the loss of a beloved, a relationship, or finances... The grief can be so strong and the losses so enormous that the ground we are walking on feels as though it is caving in. This is when it is so important to remember that we are in a process of initiation. Initiation into our deeper authenticity is one of the great gifts we can cultivate in the fertile soil of our grief. In every journey of heart and soul, there are times when we are asked to go beyond what we know. We are asked to discover something about our unique authenticity, our humanity, or about the meaning of our life that takes us beyond everything we have come to know as familiar. An initiation is a time of deep self-discovery and growth. It is a time when we can come face-to-face with ourselves, shedding whatever social masks we use to cover our authentic truth. We have a chance to unearth our deeper sense of authenticity, enriching our sense of identity and calling. Initiation is a knowledge that was held for millennia by ancient tribes and communities.

The collapse of our sturdy ground destroys many of our illusions about our own self and about life. From a larger perspective, an initiation helps us discover a deeper knowing of what our authentic personality is about—a deeper strength of real identity. The deconstruction of externally imposed mindsets can open us to our authentic gifts and calling in the world—to the deeper meaning of our life and what we value and love most. However, meaning cannot be discovered without a phase of initiation. Throughout human history, there are those who have gone through deep suffering and have listened to their suffering through open hearts. Through this suffering, they chose to seek their deeper authenticity and listen for the passion of their calling. There is nothing more important in our life than our liberated authenticity serving our true calling; this is no less than what defines our life. Our authentic calling gives us energy, passion, and presence in the world. In a sense, it is our greatest love. It is the greatest love of our spirit, because it is from this wellspring of our authenticity that we can love others and give to others. During the most difficult times of our life, we can reap the fruits of initiation. Initiation, as the psalmist David said so eloquently, is when we are going "through the valley of the shadow of death." Yet we are not losing our life. We are not alone. The valley of the shadow of death can be transmuted into a force that helps us claim our life and our calling at a much deeper and richer level. Through the process of initiation, we can arise with greater love and a more impassioned sense of direction.

The Rumi scholar and dear friend, Andrew Harvey, says it beautifully, "Out of your heartbreak comes your calling." What breaks our heart points us to what we most cherish. Trusting the deeply meaningful nature of your experience is extremely difficult, but you are being initiated into your birthright. Your grief is a powerful energy that can help you discover and liberate your unique authenticity. It can help reveal your life passion. When you choose to bravely invite these initiations into your deeper authenticity, and experience your grief consciously, respectfully, and intentionally, you grow as a human being by leaps and bounds.

All progressive visions emerge from collective grief. The greatest social movements arose from wounds that were felt and finally courageously addressed. How were protective laws for children developed if it was not for individuals who were attuned to the cries of children working themselves to death in coal mines, sweat shops, and other places? Is it not true that civil rights became a reality only when many in the U.S. felt their grief over the tragic abuse of Black Americans? Today, as we write this treatise on grief, women are loudly expressing their voices and their vision of true gender equality, for the wound of the denigration of women has become too obscene. Likewise, many are starting to look profoundly for a just policy of immigration as the previous U.S. administration ordered thousands of Latino children to be separated from their parents—deeply terrifying and traumatizing them through the process. As so many countries experience the fear of seeing their democracy stolen, the choice is between a passive caving-in or a brave-hearted initiation into an even greater vision of freedom and solidarity. Our collective anguish over the ongoing devastation of our natural environment and the harrowing development of global warming is inviting us to access the will to respond boldly and creatively. This is an inner initiation through which we free ourselves from the artificiality of social masks and the obsession of positive thinking. It is calling us to become more humanized, more powerful through our caring, stronger, and more vulnerable as we develop our ever-increasing passionate love.

This step of initiation brings nobility to our suffering. It is so easy to feel that life is betraying us when we have had one earth-shattering loss after another. All of the seminal philosophical and spiritual traditions throughout history champion the idea: "Trust your suffering. It is bringing you a sacred treasure." We are led through our grief into a deeper understanding of who we are, the true nature of our heart's calling, and our vision of social transformation. We are initiated into the depth and fullness of our own soul and the meaning and the worthiness of our presence on Earth. The key is to allow our grieving heart to speak openly to us, and for us to bravely and intelligently listen to its wisdom. Our grief has a lot to say to us, and it behooves us to neither restrain it nor hush it. Its voice, which is the voice of our own deep truth, will help us to know our heart and to focus on our vision. We will learn to discern which are the messages emerging out of an ungrounded emotional reaction, and which are authentic affirmations of our boundaries, desires, and dreams. Such discernment is essential,

I want to share the story of my dear friend Elizabeth. By the time she was 27 years old, Elizabeth had lost her stillborn son after a healthy pregnancy. Then, she and her husband became pregnant and they had a little girl named Ella, who is still with us. But a short 18 months later, her husband, Brian, was killed in Afghanistan. In that brief amount of time, Elizabeth lost her son and her husband. Her world was obliterated. When Elizabeth speaks about this period of time, she says she had no idea how she was going to breathe, how she was going to get up each morning and face the day. Out of her courageous choice and determination to transmute her suffering into meaning, Elizabeth chose to start a group for young widows called Soul Widows. She began an online support group and began offering retreats. She then joined me in opening The Respite—A Center for Grief and Hope (which sadly, despite the great work being done, had to close due to lack of funding).

In sharing her story, Elizabeth is very clear that finding her authentic way of giving back was essential in preventing being drowned in despair and bitterness and for learning more about who she was as a human being.

~ Mandy McMullen Bird

but it can only be achieved if a safe space is created for our grief to speak to us and lead us into an important initiation—an initiation into greater strength, passion, and vision.

Here are some questions for all of us: "What are we learning about our profound authentic self? Where are we being led? Where is life asking us to go? Where is life calling us? What passion is life initiating us into?" These questions are of critical importance. If we hold on to the belief that our life is isolated and does not matter, then we lose hope; and we all need hope. The world needs those who have been wounded to have hope. Their authentic and vulnerable humanity is the stuff out of which true service and true leadership are forged!

An essential tool in the grieving process is journaling. Jot down your thoughts, however unclear they may be in the beginning. With time they will become clearer. What is it that you are being initiated into and toward? What are you discovering about who you are authentically and about the authentic parts of you that have been repressed? Each time you write about it you will discover more about the transformation that your initiation is ushering into your life. Your writing will take you into a deeper understanding of the nature of your initiation.

The fact that our suffering can be transmuted ultimately into an initiation does not mean that we were meant to suffer or that suffering is a positive thing. We all suffer because we partake in the brokenness and oppression that exists in the world and in the inherent struggles of our existence. Suffering is not meant to be covered up by donning rose-colored glasses. Suffering hurts. Suffering can be debilitating. Of course, as we have said before, we want to avoid and reduce our own and others' suffering as much as possible, especially the suffering that comes from oppression. However, when we understand its initiatory potential, we can find meaning and dignity in it, and with this insight our suffering actually becomes more bearable. We have the power to extract from our suffering the soul-making gifts that intentional initiation can foster. We must understand how, as we intentionally feel our grief and engage our grief with depth and intelligence, we come to know more of our deepest self and our core desires. This is a self-knowledge at the foundation of accessing the creative force—a self-knowledge that is priceless! The initiation that our brave grieving can usher also brings us to ponder on authentic aspects of ourselves that we have neglected and will hopefully come to welcome and celebrate fully.

Another journaling suggestion is to make a list of sayings that inspire and are meaningful to you. Think of some quotes that are important to you; read and research your favorite authors and teachers. Write down their words of wisdom on post-it notes and put them in places that will remind you of wisdom and courage as you are going through your process of grieving. Keep yourself inspired. These words will give you a greater sense of dignity to help you hold your suffering.

It is so important for all of us to remember that we have been formed by the process of evolution to be people of service. We are one with the world; our spirit is hungry to find its calling. When we do not know our calling, we carry a sense of emptiness within. We disconnect from the strength in us—the force of love and creativity. This is why our calling is so important. We can fill that emptiness with any number of false replacements, but when we go through a difficult time these faulty substitutions inevitably fail us. Through times of difficulty, loss, or defeat, we have the possibility of discovering our most authentic calling. This joins us with the millions of human brothers and sisters who are trying to make a difference in the world and who are trying to build a world of justice, peace, democracy, and rebirth. By seeking to make a difference, we unleash our deepest passion and come to know the power and strength of that passion. We are people of service. Nothing can give us as much joy and fulfillment as our participation in serving our Planet Earth. Journaling and dialoguing with trusted friends or professionals can help you receive the revelation of your calling and give you a deeper and richer sense of your own life.

Another set of questions that arise for us as we go through a dark night of the soul is: "I have lost so much, how will I get it back? Will I ever get it back? Or will I live out my life diminished?" It is so important to remember that our losses can be excavated for the possibility of powerful growth and expansion of spirit. Although we might feel blinded, confused, or inwardly nauseous, we must remember there is always the choice to draw from the well of strength residing within us even when it does not feel immediately accessible. So many withdraw into numbing, abusing alcohol or drugs, or excessive and superficial socializing. They shut down and close their hearts, blocking their greater initiation. This is deeply tragic for them and for the world that loses those who could become its wounded and powerfully-human heroes. Bringing our calling out into the world demands the courage of spirit that understands and believes, "I can choose to become stronger, wiser, and more authentic through this experience."

So many people tell us that the times they have experienced significant loss, without succumbing to victimization or denial, were some of *the* most important times in their lives. Choosing to feel deeply and intensely our great grief and great joy is an incredibly effective way to counteract the destructive tendencies toward superficiality or despair. If we choose to powerfully engage and channel our authentic feelings, we will come to understand that the pain that broke our heart has meaningful offerings embedded in it. This is not just personal. Our wounding always has a collective dimension to it. We are carrying the pain of the world and by doing so we can help the world evolve. We are carrying the pain of us all—those who suffer from lies and manipulation, separation, isolation, sicknesses, the death of loved ones… those who are suffering from poverty, and children suffering in war situations or famines. All of that pain is a part of all of us, and we experience it in different circumstances and different forms. If you partake in the power of initiation to take you beyond the stark personalization of your loss, you will be in solidarity and belonging with the collective heart of all those who grieve. It is an empowered communion of tears and strong wounded hearts that enables our personality to grow to a most precious soulful depth.

Pain is never simply an individual experience. It is never only private. You may be going through it individually, but your pain is part of the pain of the world. The transformation you undertake is part of a much larger transformation. We are all in this together. As we engage in a process of transformation, we shift from being an individualistic person imprisoned in a restrictive and isolated cocoon to becoming more of a universal person—of course with a unique authentic individuality yet within a global community. There is a very important distinction between "individualism" and authentic individuality. Individualism is about the ideology of being an isolated and self-sufficient island. Authentic individuality is what we achieve through a humanizing process when our singular uniqueness of self is intrinsically tied with the well-being of others. It is when individual freedom and global solidarity become inseparable twin flames. Initiation into a deeper freedom of authenticity and a larger solidarity is sometimes very difficult. But this is the time to keep your heart open and to remember you are embarking on a (mythic) initiation. Tribal communities have been saying this for millennia: "Remember the initiation. Do not forget that your wounds can become the womb for the best in you." Allow the pain to help your spirit grow, your heart to expand, and your sense of vision to become clearer and sharper.

Your pain can either be transmuted through a life-giving and empowered initiation that strengthens and blesses you, or, if you shun and repress it, it can destructively paralyze you and end up harming your being and those you love. Grief is a moment of choice. Your choice. You can choose the nobility and the sacred nature of your pain and wring from it both blessing and strength. How you understand your pain is crucial. If you understand it as a reflection and manifestation of your noble-hearted sensitivity, your innate intelligence, and as a doorway to a generative initiation, then you will empower yourself. Of course, there will be times when you will doubt everything and feel you are barely surviving—this is part of our humanity. But you have the ability to go back, again and again, to wisdom and mine your loss and your pain as an initiation into greater self-knowing, strength, knowledge, and passion.

We have so little control over the losses that come into our life; but what we can know is that our courageous journey of initiation can deliver great passion and great blessings. It is essential that you hold your loss and your feelings of suffering within the fold of initiation; this brings dignity to your tears. You will come to a time when you will look back at what you went through and feel great pride in your courageous choices. You will know that you drank from a bitter cup and that how you held your struggle has brought you closer to the pain of others. You claimed a "grail" of becoming an agent of authenticity transformation.

We have another story to share with you about our beloved friend, Casey. She was in love with a wonderful man, Kevin, whom we all adored. Casey and Kevin had been together for eight years and, as Casey says, they worked hard for their precious relationship. They decided, after years of being together, that they wanted to get married. We were all so excited for them and we gathered together on a beautiful farm for their sweet, fun, and touching ceremony. Two weeks later Casey returned home from a trip to find Kevin dead in their bed. He, a very healthy 37-year-old, had gone to sleep and did not wake up.

We are sharing this story with you because this tragic experience became an immense initiation for Casey which we have witnessed very closely. After all those years of working so hard for their love and then Kevin's shocking death so soon after their marriage—Casey's world was blown apart. She was in excruciating pain. During the following years, she entered a profound initiation. She chose to view her tragedy as a spiritual calling and quest. She chose to believe that the result of this tragedy would bring even greater meaning into her life.

Now, Casey is delving even more deeply into ideas about authenticity, diversity, inclusion, peace, justice, and solidarity, and teaching them to others and working on developing them with us. She is touching and empowering the lives of so many through her own deep soul-power which emerged at exponential levels after the death of her dearest Kevin. She suffered an immense wound, and through her open wound, she bravely chose to mine from the wound the passion of an amazing soul leadership.

Whatever the loss that enters your life, it carries with it an invitation—one which serves the evolving consciousness of the world. When you receive that invitation, it summons you. If you look deeply, pay attention, invite your feelings to be real, and get support, you will be able to learn more and more about your deepest authentic self. You will discover your passion and how you are called to help bring greater freedom of authenticity, justice, peace, and solidarity into the world. This world needs wise individuals who have been initiated into their authentic soul passion. This is crucial.

Casey was already a spiritual coach when Kevin died. Yet it was her courageous response to his death that took her to even deeper levels of self-discovery, service, and connection with seminal ethical ideas. She chose to transmute this terrible wound into even greater depth and expanded horizons. She shared with us how viewing her painful passage through that heart-wrenching loss as an initiation saved her spirit from collapsing. She shared her journey of suffering with her community, and we offered her our support and gratitude for remaining faithful to her heart and allowing her spirit to grow immensely through this tragic time of sudden loss. As a community, we continue to thank her for what she did and is doing because we have reaped so much fruit from her tearful experience. Her grief over Kevin's death has never disappeared. She carries that wound with her for life. Yet her relationship with that wound became one of sacred respect and often a sweet and intimate friendship. We all have the opportunity, by intentionally and gracefully feeling our grief, to reconcile with who we are in the world and to fall in love even more with our authentic wounded story and destiny.

This brings us to indigenous customs and their impact on our thinking about initiation. In many tribal traditions, when one of the tribe members experiences a great loss, they are guided to find within the loss a gift to the community and a gift to themselves. The tribe then sets a special ritual to offer their thankfulness to the person for carrying the wound. This supportive gratitude is also something you can offer to yourself because you are allowing your spirit to be sculpted by, and choosing to co-create with, your loss. Be generous with yourself for the gift you are giving your community—the loss you carry will end up being a gift of greater love to others in your circle of life.

Remind yourself that you are going through a meaningful initiation by finding symbols or artwork that keep you aware of that soulful process. It could be an empty bowl that you put in a special place in your home that signifies both the emptiness you are feeling and your readiness to receive great blessings. This symbol of receptivity reminds you that right now you are being emptied, and it is that very emptiness which allows the filling. You are making yourself a vessel ready to be filled.

In addition to this symbol, a tool we recommend to help you through the deeper exploration of your initiation is the art of collage. Gather together images that are meaningful to *you* of a soul-passage and profound transformation. These images can be from the internet, magazines, or ones you create yourself. Use a piece of heavy art paper or light cardboard and place the images together. Use an image of a bridge (or something similar) to express the idea of reaching a further shore of yourself. Experiment with the arrangement and try many configurations. There will be a particular grouping that just "feels right" as an expression of your initiation. Affix the images in this arrangement and keep it somewhere close by so you can turn to it often and explore the symbolic and personal meaning of your collage. The collage will be a powerful mirror for you—revealing how your wise and intentional grieving is initiating you toward parts of yourself longing to be freed and toward a vision of greater service.

In summary, initiation is about a brave delving into your deeper authentic identity, passion, and calling. In this chapter, we have addressed three questions: "How will I come out of this grief?" "How will I recover everything I have lost?" and "Where am I heading?" The answers to these questions encompass the gifts of a greater knowing of one's authentic self and calling, a greater capacity to love, and a larger vision of what your life is about. This vision includes a larger vista of love and care, a deep sense of justice, and commitments to global peace, individual authenticity, and inclusion.

The world today is in a very difficult place, and our collective grief needs to be felt so visions of evolutionary transformation can arise. If we fail to feel this collective grief, we will not be initiated into the sharp awareness which comes with possible solutions or be able to respond powerfully to the crises we face. However, if we open our eyes to our collective wounds and refuse despair and cynicism, then we can become visionary pioneers. Ecologically, conservation and more sustainable practices are an inescapable requirement. Economically, the situation is seriously challenging. We are witnessing a concentration of super wealth in the hands of the very few while a completely unacceptable level of poverty continues and even broadens. We have roughly half-a-billion children living in dire poverty. Fundamentalism and its violence are spreading around the world displacing millions of innocent people. Authoritarian supra-wealthy individuals want to replace democracy with systems of control and domination. The Earth is calling out for people who have faced and bravely mined their wounds for a love that is powerful and profound and who are ready to be passionate about serious steps toward global solidarity. The Earth is calling out for people who have accessed a wisdom beyond social superficiality and a strength beyond surrendered resignation—people who are renewed and whose minds are reborn through the suffering they have endured.

We are in dire need of people in every city, every country, every culture, and every spiritual tradition to become socially and ecologically engaged for the purpose of making a significant and lasting difference—a difference from their authentic heart. Only those who have known pain in their own life and allowed this pain to enrich their life with dignity and compassion can make this type of powerful difference in the world. Those who have known grief empathize with the grief of others. Those who have suffered oppression or loss know compassion for others who have suffered oppression and loss. This is what remaining authentically genuine does. The world needs the passion arising from the truth of our broken and open hearts.

In my early thirties I started reading the work of the mythologist Joseph Campbell on the topic of initiation. [Campbell studied myths and rituals of every major religion, modern and ancient.] He demonstrated how the idea of the heroic initiation—when an individual comes to know their deeper life task through their suffering—is at the core of all spiritual stories. Through Campbell's work I realized I had found something I could hold on to. His research and heroic perspective helped me understand that when I am deeply wounded, I have a choice to *not* see my wounding as a total devastation and loss of hope. I learned to hold it as possibility for an initiation into a deeper and richer dimension of my being and power. When so much was collapsing in my youth and early adulthood, when I felt like I was spiraling down with no bottom in sight and felt that

(Continued in next box)

life was turning against me, Campbell's writing about initiation allowed me to stay as centered as possible throughout the wrenching difficulties. It gave meaning and worth to my suffering and offered a light at the end of the tunnel. It upheld the dignity of my pain and called me to a higher courage and purpose. It gave me a taste of how I could both love more and love more boldly. It provided me with a sense of the sacredness of my wounds. I felt an abiding power in my heart no matter the circumstances I was facing.

The truth is, that every time I have been through a strong challenge of pain, there have been moments of despair. But I learned that I have to go back to my source of wisdom—my center—and keep my heart open and alive. It was very hard for me to hold on to the promise that in the midst of collapse there was a treasure, especially when the loss was getting bigger and bigger. Recently, I have been challenged with chronic and very intense migraines. They are often debilitating. I have to remind myself almost daily that with the disability and very real losses these migraines bring, there are great gifts for me to mine from them. I am choosing to embark on another important initiation in my life that will engage me in discovering even more about my deep authenticity and my soul task ahead. I have to stay aware and intentional. I can tell you now, that when I look back at my life, there has not been a single time when I experienced a great loss that when I chose to mine it, I did not receive manifold blessings as well.

As long as I stayed faithful to my heart and allowed myself to move into the deeper authenticity, strength, and vision, the initiation has always ultimately been life-giving. When I listened to my heart and listened through my heart, my creative passion grew. This does not mean that everything became easy (like much of pop spirituality asserts things will if you just "think positive"). But it does mean that I was able to enrich my life with meaning, passion, and strength through

(Continued in next box)

the hard challenges.

I could mostly free myself of stress because I learned to be at peace with my story, my wounds, my grief, my defeats, my successes, and my hope—I learned to be at peace with it all!

~ Chris Saade

I was already living out my leadership and going for my calling when I got the voicemail from Chris telling me that our close friend Kevin had died (the story shared a few pages ago). It was a mere three weeks after their wedding date that we reassembled back at the same farm where Casey and Kevin had been married to participate in his memorial service, to tell him goodbye, and to celebrate his spirit. I thought to myself, "This is it! No more playing small." I have had many losses in my own life—a divorce, many other griefs and struggles, and with Kevin's death, I just thought, "What am I doing? What am I doing to bring my gifts to the world? Where are my gifts taking me? Where are they calling me to serve in a greater way for justice, for peace, for compassion, for inclusion, for those who need help and hope to know that there are practical tools that can profoundly help in the journey through grief?"

It was through my conscious engagement with those moments of pain and loss that I was able to discover a new level of power and urgency to pursue those callings fueled by the experience of having my heart broken open again.

~ Mandy McMullen Bird

Step Four: Paradox

Learn to fully experience the paradoxical aspects of your authentic feelings (grief and joy). Honor both rivers of feeling that flow in you—thus experiencing the fullness of life.

Befriend your wounds as well as the sources of your joy. They are both the essential colors of the canvas of your soul.

This step of heart-centered grief and hope is about understanding and embracing the great wisdom of paradox to help you experience grief in a healthy and empowered way. Living with paradox is learning how to hold feelings which are very different yet complimentary. All feelings are life-giving. They are all natural and authentically human. When held together, they ground us, strengthen us, and give us a complete and genuine experience of life.

Let us start by making it clear that paradox and contradiction are not the same and need to be differentiated. Paradox must never be used to describe destructive contradictions. For example, someone who says, "I love you, but I don't respect you," is not speaking a paradox but rather a blatant contradiction. However, to say, "I am happy to be with you, and I am disappointed in something you did," is expressing real and life-giving paradoxical feelings. Contradictions break us down, while paradoxes enrich us.

We are well served to remember that life comes to us in an endless stream of paradoxes: roses have a wonderful fragrance and are also very fragile and full of thorns; rain is refreshing and necessary for the soil and can also leave us drenched and cold. The world is amazing, yet also anguishing. Our personal story is graced with successes and defeats. So it is with feelings: we have joy and sorrow, peace and outrage, excitement and anxiety. These paradoxical feelings are continuously flowing in us, though one may be more prominent depending on the situation. Life is rich in paradoxes.

Learning to experience grief while remaining connected to the other side of the paradox means holding our deep sorrow, anxiety, and anger, while remembering our happiness, excitement, and peace—both sides of the whole, all residing within us at the same time.

Experiencing our grief through a larger paradox brings us energy and comfort. It encourages us and nourishes our soul. If we only feel our grief without accessing our joy, excitement, or peace, we weaken ourselves and become vulnerable to victimization and paralyzing despair. This is not about negating the truth and integrity of our grief. Actually, the more we stand in the paradox, the more we can feel our grief without the fear of it drowning us.

When life hurts, life also has joy for us. Learning to hold our grief paradoxically means that when something difficult, painful, or tragic happens in our life we grieve—yet without losing out on the beauty of life in its fullness. Labeling our experience as *only* sad or tragic robs us of the other side of the paradox: happiness, peace, and excitement. Holding on to only the depth of our sorrow and suffering without allowing ourselves to feel the other side of our joy can easily take us to a place of hopelessness.

Imagine an eagle with its magnificent wing span—two strong wings that represent both sides of life—grief and joy. Imagine the balance and power of these wings and the necessity of both being spread wide for soaring. Now, imagine your own suffering and your own blessings of happiness as the foundational balance in your life. This is your flight through life. Fly with both wings spread out, each its own but connected through the heart-center. This will enable you to stay centered and moving forward. This is an invitation to feel, experience, and invite fully and equally, grief and joy—both sides of an essential paradox that teaches us so much about the fullness of who we are.

An important question that is asked and should be asked is: "How do I avoid getting utterly lost in my grief and losing all perspective?" This is a critical question because our greatest fear is that if we descend into our grief, we will get lost in it. We are afraid we will drown in our own sadness. This is a fear we all share—a normal fear. This is why embracing paradox is so important. Like an eagle soaring through the sky, we must move into our grief with both wings spread in order to be able to experience both the fullness and profundity of our sadness while remaining tethered to the deep joy that is also an inextricable part of our authentic existence. They might be small joys initially, but the ability to feel both grief and joy allows us not to be overtaken by despair. As human beings we have the ability to experience and embody all aspects of our life. It behooves us to remain conscious about the fullness of life in which we partake. We need to be intentional about calling forth happy memories and peaceful feelings while our heart is broken. This practice is very salutary, and it is a crucial tool for helping us be in our grief without drowning in it.

There is a distinction between fully experiencing our grief and being taken over by that grief. If we are taken over by our grief, we lose all sense of perspective. But when we are able, like the eagle, to center ourselves and spread both wings, we gain the ability to have our tears *and* to also have smiles and laughter, not always in equal measure but always present. The fullness of our humanity and of life is here.

We are made to experience the fullness of the paradox. Our human psyche is able to experience many feelings at the same time. Many people have been able to experience overwhelming losses without losing their bearings, because they maintained the integrity of paradox in their lives. Many of our clients and trainees have confirmed the centering power they experienced by claiming the fullness of the paradox even when their challenges felt overwhelming. For example, one client who had gone through extremely traumatic experiences shared how she was able, along with and through her tears and sorrow, to notice a little flower breaking through the concrete. Although she was going through a trauma, she was able to see the incredible beauty of that flower and to feel nurtured by that observation. Many have practiced truly noticing their child's smile and allowing that to nurture them even as they struggled inwardly. This is how our psyche maintains its integrity and its power. Our psyche is very large. It contains all of our feelings. Sometimes we believe that we only have room to feel the sadness that we are shouldering, but the reality is that if we could x-ray our psyche, we would see a lot of different feelings all at the same time. As human beings, we are a reflection of the world, and the world is a reflection of our psyche. There is a lot of pain and grief in the world. There are a lot of struggles and challenges. But there is also a lot of joy and beauty. The world has never existed without both pain and joy. The reality is always the paradox of both. By aligning ourselves with this paradoxical reality of losses and gifts, sorrows and joys, we become strong and empowered.

Every day, life gifts us the beautiful sunshine or a gorgeous sunset—a moment of beauty in one form or another. Life is filled with people caring and giving us attention or affection. Life also contains personal and collective losses. The invitation is to stay aware of the fullness of our being even during the most difficult times of our life. It is also wise to remember that in many spiritual traditions the heart of the Divine, the heart of God, is also seen as being fully paradoxical. These traditions speak about how one side of the heart of the Divine holds incredible bliss—filled with eternal beauty and joy; and the other part of the heart of the Divine is broken—broken and in tears over the suffering in the world. The Divine Mother or the Divine Father is in tears over the children who are suffering, over the animals who are howling in pain, over the devastated Earth, and over global injustice and oppression. When we are in deep grief, it is difficult to keep the paradox in our awareness, but this is exactly when we need to keep it in mind. To be able to integrate grief in a healthy and meaningful way, we need to keep the consciousness of joy alive as well.

There is a special method of journaling that is of immense help when we are faced with times in our life that are frightening and challenging. It is called two-sided journaling. Divide a page in your journal in half by drawing a line straight down the middle. On the left side of the page, write all that is sorrow and grief, all that is creating anxiety or anger. On the right side of the page, write about the beauty in your life, all that you are grateful and happy for, excited or deeply peaceful about. Use different colors of ink for each side of the page if you can.

By filling in as much as possible on the two sides of your journal, you spread out your two wings. Try to write an almost equal amount about each so the weight is balanced as much as possible. If you are carrying a huge grief, then write about many small joys or places where you find and enjoy beauty. Keep going until you intuitively feel you have awakened and fully expanded the two sides. Even though the grief will still be very much with you, you have built a paradoxical container for it. Sometimes it will take you a while to fully awaken and balance the two wings, especially if the loss is absolutely heart-breaking like the loss of a child or an extreme sickness. You might have to stretch slowly into the other wing step-by-step, accepting the severity of your pain, but always remembering that there is something, or some people, in your life who warm your heart. Remembering is the key. Again, this is not about thinking positively about or diminishing our grief and trying to deny it. Rather it is about respecting its integrity while joining it to the other wing of beauty and gratitude that is *also* true in our life. The more we can hold both sides, each in their own integrity, the more we can feel the passion growing out of our tears.

Another practical tool to help in this step of paradox is to go to a museum and view artwork representing both sorrow and joy. There is such a wide, encompassing variety of paintings, sculptures, and other artworks that portray people grieving as well as celebrating. Grief and joy expressed through the beauty of art is universal. Spending time with these paintings, sculptures, and other forms of art is an opportunity to reflect upon the totality of our grief experience—its suffering, and its beauty.

The idea of paradox is very bold because it can be misinterpreted as being insensitive to the depth of our pain. Deep sorrow and emotional pain often feel overwhelming to your body, mind, and spirit. Choosing to feel and acknowledge the good things in your life can feel disloyal to the grief, yet the truth is that honoring our paradoxical feelings is life-saving. We are not suggesting that you replace grief with joy while you are mourning—one should never replace the other. It is about claiming the stabilizing fullness of your heart by accessing the other side of life. It is about the other energy in life (joy and pleasure) which we need even more intensely when we are deeply hurting. Paradox actually honors our grief because it sets it in the container of the full reality of life.

You might say: "I do not feel any gratitude or excitement right now. How can I feel joy?" We had to learn to intentionally experience paradox when we are challenged by overwhelming grief. We have to remember that we have all the feeling-energies available to us at all times. Some might need to be accessed intentionally and manually. It is not simple. It means choosing to authentically dig deep to find the other side. But when we are successful, we feel empowered and free of despair and victimization while still honoring our grief. We feel strong through our grief.

Our spirit always experiences the world in paradox. We can learn to reach deeper and deeper into our own authenticity. We cannot move toward our calling if we do not experience all of our feelings while affirming our grief. You cannot reclaim your life force and your passion without calling on both sides of your feelings.

If you are not willing to stretch and reach for whatever it is that brings you a sense of peace, a sense of happiness, and a sense of excitement in life, you risk losing your ability to feel and hold your grief and thus your ability to mine it for its great gifts. You might sink into depression or rage, which are not grief. Think about driving a stick-shift car and the experience of manually moving from one gear to the next. While grieving, you have to intentionally (manually) remember and feel your sources of joy and invite in the fullness of your truth in order to stay empowered. If you only (and the key word here is *only*) stay focused on your sadness, anger, and anxiety, you will spiral down into despair. Life can seem hopeless. That is why it is *so* important to learn how to reach for the other side—to feel both sides and to shift your inner gears manually.

Accessing the other side of your feelings when you are hurting helps you fight off paralysis. The tool is to claim the fullness of your paradoxical feelings: the paradox of grief and joy. While mourning, feel your love for others and their love for you. Allow yourself to really enjoy that morning cup of coffee, talk to your children, meet with a friend, read a good book, go for a run—whatever it is that helps you embrace paradox. Accessing the other side of grief gives you footing, and grounds you in your strength. Remember that grief alone does not cause depression. We know this. But depression can be triggered by two things: one, the suppression of grief, or two, a victimized mentality arising from not keeping joy, excitement, or peace within sight while we are grieving. In other words, we suffer if we fail to keep *both* paradoxical wings of our eagle-spirit spread wide.

Each morning when you wake up, name a gift or blessing in your life. The important thing is to have an internal dialogue that honors what brings you peace, joy, or excitement. Then call, email, or text a trusted friend and share this in addition to sharing your grief (not instead of your grief). Do this as a daily ritual. Name your grief, as well as your joy, and share them both. This acknowledgement of blessing will help you stay centered and grounded in your grief. If some days you are too sad to reach to the other side, be gentle with yourself. You can always try again the next day—but trying even in small incremental steps makes a big difference.

Life is not limited to joy, peace, or excitement; life is all of it, sometimes all at once. Life is also moments of anger against injustice, moments of collective outrage against oppression, and tremendous anxiety about the future of democracy in the world. Love life. Go for all of life. Remember that living is always about the richness and complexity of life. Be fully human. Refuse to be limited to any one feeling. Even the falsely named "positive" feelings become destructive if they are severed from the paradox of life and from our full humanity. There are no negative or positive feelings, only destructive or life-giving behaviors.

This leads us to another extremely important question: "Will my memories of joy block me from experiencing my grief?" The deep truth is that the more joy you access, the deeper you can go into the soul and heart of your grief. Accessing joy when you are going through your grief is not about denial. Some people use an unhelpful (and emotionally dangerous) form of positive thinking to block their grief by saying, "Oh everything is going well. Look at the beautiful sunshine out there. Look at all the beautiful smiles in the world. Look at the house I have," and so on, as a way to deny their grief. This is precisely what we do *not* want to do. Grief must not be denied. Grief must be experienced; it is a sacred initiation in your life. You cannot avoid grief. If you try to deny it, it will turn into depression. So-called "positive thinking" that diverts us from grief cuts us off from life and robs us of our precious humanity and authentic connection with others. Instead of denying and avoiding the reality of your grief, invite the paradox so you can have both wings available to you.

Life begets life. The more you allow the fullness of life to move through you, the more abundant your life is. The deeper your genuine grief, the deeper your genuine joy. Joy opens the heart like grief opens the heart. It is interesting to note that people who try to remain in a "middle place" of not feeling too much grief, are also unable to feel a lot of joy. If your heart is not open, it will not be able to feel full joy, nor the full power of love and passion. If your heart is open, you will feel grief and the sensitivity of empathy. That is how life is. What allows us to feel and experience all of life deeply is the heart being open and alive. The truth is that our heart will be impacted over and over again throughout our time on Earth. This is a sign of aliveness. The heart that breaks upon seeing an elder in the community who is isolated, exiled, lonely, and without support, is the same heart that will see the blooming tree and flowers in the spring. It is the same heart that can deeply feel love and be passionate about relationships, physical intimacy, and meaningful projects or causes. We need to get away from the idea that somehow joy might (or should) suppress grief. This is not the case. Joy needs to accompany the reality of our grief. The more joy you bring in your life, the more you will be able to feel, respect, and honor the authenticity of your grief. But you will be carrying your grief with the *fullness of your being* and the *fullness of your presence*, without limiting yourself. You now have the knowledge of the paradox—how both grief and joy nurture and need each other for life and love to thrive.

An additional tool to help hold paradox is to use a sideways figure 8. First draw a sideways figure 8, then color half of that sideways figure 8 with the color of grief. It could be gray, red, or whatever feels right for you. Next, color the other half of the figure 8 with the color of joy. Trace your figure 8 from the grief side into joy and back again. Get a sense of how you can flow from grief to joy and from joy to grief. Let that drawing remind you that you are always in *all* of life. Think about the two sides of the paradox as partners, dancing and flowing back and forth. It is so important to learn how to flow back and forth between both energies, without suppressing either, so we can stay balanced and feel empowered in our humanity.

As you learn how to hold your grief paradoxically—with that wide, expansive, two-winged perspective—you will discover that you are much stronger than you have ever believed yourself to be! You are a full being, even during the darkest times in your life. Your spirit is whole. You always have joy and blessings in your life, no matter how big your grief. You are never diminished. The spirit in you pulses and thrives with all of life, all of the time. As you go through the sacred initiation of grief, know that all of life resides in you. Sometimes you have to shift gears manually to find the joy and the hope—but they are always there. The fullness of life is always present within you at every moment.

Grief is the twin sister of joy. This reality—that life is indeed paradoxical at every moment—opens up to us an entirely new world. When joy and grief dance together in every area of our life, we do not have to fight so hard to accept and honor our selves. The more we are able to experience our grief, the more we are able to experience our joy, and the other way around. This is the true condition of our reality: the *paradoxical fullness* of our feelings is something to embrace and respect. The more we can feel all of our feelings, the more we can be awake and alive to the fullness of our own being. Happiness and grief are dancing partners.

In ancient Phoenicia, in the Mediterranean where Lebanon is now, it was said that when great grief meets great joy and they walk hand-in-hand, then together they can call on the experience of ecstatic celebration. It is a request that life cannot resist. But the condition is that the hands of grief and joy must be held together tightly, honestly, and with intensity.

Intimacy in relationships is also greatly enhanced by the respectful sharing of both grief and joy. Intimacy is deepened and sweetened by treating grief as a communion of souls through which we support each other in our woundedness. Of course, the other complementary and propelling force of intimacy in our relationships is the mutual sharing of vibrancy and unabashed joy. It is important to create a space in our relationship to talk of our excitement as well as our sorrows, both with mutual respect, otherwise we deprive the relationship of a rich human intimacy. Without the sharing of paradoxical feelings, the union of two individuals will not be impassioned. Without both wings of the paradox, a relationship will get mired in an artificial silence bereft of life and vitality. Such a loss of humanity and intimacy in the relationship will significantly weaken both the emotional and the sexual bond. Our partners and our friends need to be fed with the tender vulnerability of our being as well as the flowing waters of our joy. We need this essential double-nourishment from each other.

Many new approaches to spirituality are very disempowering and dehumanizing as they advocate the splitting and tamping down of joy and grief. This separation is hugely problematic. First, it disregards the deep wisdom of the ancient traditions that embrace joy and grief as two sides of the same paradoxical coin. Second, denying our grief makes unadulterated joy impossible. Third, when divorced from grief, happiness often becomes an inauthentic mask we wear which causes us to lose our humanity and act artificially. And fourth, joy that is untethered from its twin grief is unsustainable.

Lastly, a spiritual teaching that disconnects joy and grief is not healthy for us, nor is it good for the world. The severing of joy and grief can induce a blindness to the suffering that is all around us. Those deprived of their rights and dignity need our deeply felt empathy. We need to understand how important it is to build collective relationships through sharing whatever grief is real and present in our heart. We need to learn how to grieve together.

I can tell you from the losses I have experienced—whether it was suffering in my childhood or in my adult life—I have been able to garner deeper wisdom and clarity about myself and the work I am called do. This calling to help people dive into their authenticity and claim the lives that they want for themselves would never have been revealed to me without each experience. The passion I have to help others claim the nobility of their grief and learn the rich paradox of their grief and joy comes from my own painful experiences and my own journey toward claiming the truth of both sides of the paradox in my life.

~ Mandy McMullen Bird

I want to share the story of a woman I was working with who touched me very deeply. She was in her late 70's and she had cancer, a very tough and difficult cancer. She was already a widow and her children had moved out of town just six months before she was diagnosed. At times she would say that everything felt dark, that there was no more light left in her world. She had remained semi-depressed for quite a long time. We worked a lot on the co-existence of joy and grief. One day she looked outside her window and saw new growth happening in her garden and she said, "I am experiencing tremendous loss and tremendous grief, but life is still growing. Life is still alive and so beautiful in so many ways." She decided to put up pictures of people, places, and things that she really enjoyed in a special place. Then she made it a point that before and after doing her grief work, she would go and look at these pictures and be reminded about the great joys that still existed in her life. She came to realize how life is bigger than any one feeling. She honored her tears and brought them to be accompanied by beautiful memories that made her heart smile, even in that most difficult grief process of hers.

~ Chris Saade

I was sitting outside on a gorgeous day and found it quite amusing that a hummingbird continued to zoom around where I was sitting. (The hummingbird is the Native American totem for joy.) This brought a huge smile to my face. The beautiful message I took in that moment was a great reminder from the Divine, from God, and from the Universe saying to us all, "Seek joy. Go after joy. Discover your delights and pleasure." We become exhausted without joy. We hurt too much without joy. We are imbalanced without joy. Joy is the sister of grief, and we need joy's huge arms wrapped around us to hold us and solidify us in the fullness of life. Wherever we are or whatever we are doing, there is something joyous available for us even in the most difficult circumstances. From grand magnificent things like a gorgeous sky or sunset, to small benign things that we may celebrate, like a sweet memory or a good cup of tea or coffee. Learning to access our joy during times of great struggle is a skill that can save our lives and bless those we love.

~ Mandy McMullen Bird

This I have learned: when I call forth joy to accompany my grief, then I can hold my grief without falling into victimization. I had a very rough childhood. I lived through seven years of war in Lebanon; I went through divorce; I had difficult sicknesses; I had friends who were killed by the senseless violence of the war; I lost my wealth during the war; I lost my home and my country of origin—yet through it all I kept on experiencing the beauty in the world through a paradoxical consciousness of the twin rivers of grief and joy. My wounds were shockingly real, and my grief was genuine··· and there was still beauty all around me. Love still existed, so did tenderness. I remember one day feeling extremely distraught. It was when I sought refuge in France after I had lost everything in Lebanon. I saw a mother walking towards me with the cutest little boy. He was

(Continued in next box)

probably two or three years old and he looked at me and started making ugly faces. I thought, "Why are you making faces at me? Do you not realize how fragile I am here?" Then, all of the sudden he gave me this huge smile. I was thinking how exhausted I was. But I was able to smile back. We looked at each other as new friends, even if it was for a moment. That young preschooler taught me about joy in a split second on the sidewalk. The reality is that life makes faces at me and smiles at me and wants to be funny with me and to give me joy all through the times of my grief and independent from the reasons for my grief.

When I can remember to grieve full-heartedly and feel my wounds full-heartedly, and at the same time realize that there is the possibility of immense joy all around me—nurturing me, supporting me, waiting for me, and compelling me—then I feel sadness without experiencing victimization. I feel grief without dis-empowerment. This has been extremely important in my life.

As we face the global ecological crisis we are in, the problems with acts of terrorism around the world, the accumulation of wealth in the hands of the few corporate giants, and the threats against democracy, it is very important to know how to hold our grief without being victimized individually or collectively. I need to feel my grief and my anguish without losing my determination to create, write, and speak. Yes, I will shed tears, but I will shed them with strength and with the knowledge that life is not only made of tears. Life reminds me often about the mystery and magnificence of presence—through the grief, through the joy, and through the love that dances with our tears and our joys.

~ Chris Saade

Step Five: Spiritual Fortitude

Let your own heart-spirituality be the sturdy and supportive container of your grief.

As you grieve, connect with the greater force within you—the force that emanates from a well deep in you that is connected to what is beyond the immediate.

Our heart-centered grieving is empowered when we ground ourselves in spiritual fortitude. It is an invitation to let your spirituality be the sturdy and supportive container of your grief. When we go through times that are demanding and difficult, when we feel that we can no longer carry the grief that is part of our life, that is the time to focus on the deep spiritual presence within us that can hold our sorrow and much more. It is about the presence of the Sacred as each of us personally defines it; it is spirituality as you experience it in your life—whether it is Christ, or Buddha, or Nature, or the Universe, or your Greater Power.

It is true that there are moments of intense grief which no individual can hold in their entirety. This is precisely why it is so important to find the center of spiritual presence within us that can help us hold our immense grief. We need to remind ourselves that there is something much bigger inside us that can uphold us in our vulnerability through the most difficult of times. It is crucial that we remember that the force of love resides in us. It is also very important not to personalize grief, not to make it only about us, because then it becomes unbearable. It is essential to remember that our grief is part of the grief of the world, an experience we partake of through love with others.

When we are in intense emotional pain and deeply suffering, our tendency is to want to get out of our body. Spiritual fortitude is about learning to deeply immerse ourselves within our own center as a way of finding the strength to stay in our body and in touch with what is real. We allow this solid foundation and these deep spiritual roots to buttress us, so we are actually able to enter our body more deeply and experience within our mind and heart the strength to weather our grief through this spiritual partnership. It is about deepening the inner force. In other words, spiritual fortitude means finding the inner unbreakable fortress where we work in partnership with the Divine to help us bear the losses in our life, so we can keep mining the precious gifts in our wounds.

Losses present us with the big question: "Where can I find the strength to hold my profound sadness and still live a full life without denying my losses?" This question obliges us to look for our deepest well of strength. Spiritual fortitude enables us to feel our grief honestly and know that we have, within the deeper part of our center, the power to weather every storm. Spiritual fortitude introduces us to the largeness of who we really are. It gives us an unexpected strength to move through our most difficult questions and circumstances. This is one of the gifts we mine from our grief, our wounds, and our losses: knowing the greater power that resides in us and how to access it to build a sturdier character—a character more grounded in love and the bold generosity of love's passion.

As we dive into our center, we find safety in our partnership with the Sacred. We hear the invitation to partake in the grief of the world and become part of the creative and compassionate solutions the world needs. We come to realize that we can draw on a force hidden during the winters of life. We come to see that we are more powerful in our vulnerability than we ever thought—that within our woundedness there is a stunning strength, ever ready to burgeon into new possibilities.

Spiritual fortitude gives us the power to initiate a respectful dialogue with our grief—to allow grief to speak fully to us. We seek and claim the wisdom held within the chambers of our grief. The discovery of such wisdom will come in steps and at different levels at different times, but our grief has a lot to offer to us. As we tend to our grief, we can learn a lot, not only about what to avoid, but also about our deepest authenticity, stronger character, love, passion, and the meaning of our life.

A practical tool to help implement this idea is to create some kind of artistic rendering—any kind. It can be a collage, a drawing, a painting, a sculpture. It doesn't have to be "good"—just authentic! Create an image symbolizing the Source of life or the Divine, and then draw a larger circle around it representing the world in its struggles and grief. Put your heartbreak in the center to be held by the Sacred, and then connect it to the larger circle of the world's grief. Visualize the sacred nature of your greatest heartbreak. See how your grief is tenderly and respectfully held by the Sacred. See how your grief is part of the larger ocean of our collective grief, and how it ultimately contributes to a collective transformation.

One woman created a circle of stones representing her losses and her grief. Within that circle she placed a beautiful big stone representing the Divine as ultimately stronger than any pain. Then she created an outer circle representing her connection with the grief of the world and the understanding that we are an intrinsic part of the Universe.

This creative tool can be used to remind us that we are not alone. We are connected to a greater source of strength. We are also one with the collective human story. We can remind ourselves of this important connection through the personal creative expressions which symbolize our universal connection. This creative representation—whether it is on paper, in the garden, or takes on some other form—will constantly remind us of the connection we have with the divine center and with all those around us who are one with us in their struggles and hopes.

A frequent question for those who believe in a greater power is, "How can I get closer to God or the divine Source when my heart is broken, when I am so distraught?" This is such an important question, as is the answer. God is the closest to you when you are broken in grief, like a mother is closest to her child when the child is in pain. Remember that there is no time that God is closer to you than when tears overwhelm you and when your heart cries out its loss and its pain.

It is spiritual fortitude that empowers you to say "YES!" to life. It is a faith that says, "No matter what, and despite it all, I will say 'YES!'" And it is a heroic "YES!" because it is not easy. When we say this epic "YES!" we are ultimately walking hand-in-hand with the Sacred and working to create a world of greater peace and freedom, a world of justice, a world of inclusion, and a world of solidarity, despite all the challenges. And today more than ever we need individuals who have that level of serious care and passion.

We get closer to the Source of life by understanding that the Sacred is ultimately about love. The best aspects of different spiritual traditions teach us that divine love is unbounded. This great love is there for every suffering child in the world. It is there for every person who is put down, insulted, or abused. By opening our heart to love, we encompass suffering; we open ourselves to the divine love that flows through us and out to others who are suffering in the world, to those who are seeking justice and peace, to those who are craving compassionate solidarity and praying to be included. We become greater containers of love as well as givers of that love.

By allowing love to flow through us, especially when we feel broken ourselves, we sense the Sacred even more. When we personalize our own problems by limiting our experience to ourselves, we shrink and lose our sense of power and connection. Love is unbounded. This sense of the largeness of love—the realization that our brokenness opens us to becoming vessels that allow love to flow through us to the world—allows us to get closer and closer to the Sacred and the universal. The heart opens so it can love more—love for our significant partner, love for our children (all children!), love for the world, love for the poor, love for the noble-hearted in our world who are struggling, love for those who are experiencing oppression, love for women who are mistreated, love for people who are isolated because of their sexual orientation… Remember that the Sacred resides in your grief and in your most generous love.

Another very helpful tool here is to write your own words of spiritual encouragement. Explore the meaning of your pain through writing your own spiritual wisdom and read it regularly. It is too easy to forget all that we know when times are difficult and stressful. Write about your grief in its greater connection to the Sacred and to the world. Write about the ways in which God or the Sacred loves you passionately and grieves with you. Write about the profound meaning of your grief and the ways it has gifted you, strengthened you, and enriched your love. Write the words that inspire you and help you experience the power of your spiritual fortitude. These words must be fierce and encouraging. As you read them and look at relevant images that you have collected, they will make the experience of the Sacred supporting you feel more tangible and real. Use this tool to become more grounded in the power of love that sustains you and defines the beauty of your spirit.

It is common for those who are suffering great loss to experience feeling confused and blinded. "As I am going through intense grief, I feel unable to see anything as a gift or as meaningful, and I become so confused. I feel disconnected and cut off." Opening yourself to spiritual revelation will help you see your way through this blindness. You will have to trust what is moving through your depth. Listen to it and explore it respectfully. You will be led, your spiritual fortitude will rise, and the dense fog will break away. Your partnership with a sacred power—with a power of love—will reframe, enrich, and inspire your new vision of life.

It is when you are struggling the most that you have the opportunity to buckle down and seek even more deeply—ask all types of questions, refuse to give up, and turn over every single stone in your quest. You will be on your path toward the realization that no matter what is being taken away, no matter how frightening it feels, greater gifts are coming to you through your brave encountering and creative responding to your wound.

Another tool that can help very much is receptive prayer or listening (especially combined with journaling). Receptive prayer is a time when you are totally silent and create a space within yourself to receive revelation. It is not a time when you are talking to God or speaking your needs and desires (although that is very important too). It is a time when you are totally silent and listening to what is coming through you, listening to what is emerging from the depth of your heart. After this period of receptive prayer, go to your journal and record the images and insights that came to you. Let them flow without censorship. This does not mean that everything that comes through is something you will want to hold on to, but you will find many incredible gems. You will find revelations that you could only receive because you are deeply listening through the confusion and pain of your loss. Using receptive prayer, you will be able to take in information, images, and insights which will guide you and empower you. Remember that the wound always releases creative energy. If you look closely, you will see that your grief is flooding your imagination with new and very rich images. This is a time to sit in silence, receive, and then record—either in writing or through recording yourself verbally if you prefer. You will be astonished at how much will come to you. It is actually through our blindness that we can begin to see the deeper revelations of our own spirit.

One woman we know who had suffered many profound losses was deeply committed to her journaling. As she wrote, she recognized that her sense of blindness and isolation was beginning to dissipate. She came to realize that she needed to love and affirm her authentic self much more intensely and take her calling even more seriously (in her case it was a calling to go back to school and study the history of racial discrimination against Hispanics and other minorities). She began to see the world in a very different light—a world in which her calling really mattered. She could see how she was paradoxically connected to everyone around her through all that had been taken away from her. This strong connection with the world was a new feeling for her, and she reveled in this shift and sought to embody it.

In summary, in this step of spiritual fortitude, the questions we have explored are: "How can I get closer to God through my grief?" And "How can I see God's guidance when I feel blind?" The essential things to remember are that you are never alone and that within your grief are burgeoning power and passion. You are one with the Sacred, and you are one with the world. We are unique individuals, and we are also individuals who are part of a greater tapestry—it is this authentic belonging which empowers us.

In your inner fortress, you know that your spiritual fortitude can be more powerful than any wound. So always remember that however strong the pain is, there is always a greater blessing. There is growth. There is calling. There is opportunity. There is passion emerging. There is transformation when we walk with the Sacred keeping an open heart and caring for the world. When we access that inner sanctuary and know that the Divine is there to partner with us, we discover hope and the courage to seek out our own sacred task.

In indigenous tribal stories, there is a wonderful ritual around grief. Specific members of the tribe create a sacred space surrounded by beautiful large stones. When a person is in deep grief, they are able to visit that sacred space. It is a physical embodiment that honors grief as a powerful transformative experience. In this tradition, grief is perceived and honored as a sacred process. However painful, our brave engagement with grief makes us stronger, wiser, more human, and more compassionate. This heroic dance multiplies our passion and emboldens the love force in us. Grief is not just something that happens to us; it is part of a much bigger story to which we belong.

The human journey has progressed through great challenges, and through those difficulties and tragedies we have courageously accessed greater creativity in how we face and respond to these challenges. This is how we have evolved as a human race as well as individuals. We face huge challenges that feel as though they will break us, then we realize that we are connected to a greater power—a Source that enables us to birth the passions of freedom and love.

I want to share with you another personal story about surviving the aftereffects of the war in Lebanon. I came to the United States and started a new life. I was also doing a lot of therapeutic exploration around all the losses I had incurred. I was still so angry with God about the children who I saw suffering in the war. I would say to God, "How can you be a God of love and let the children suffer so atrociously?" Their suffering, regardless of whether they were Christian, Muslim, or Jewish, tore my heart asunder. I remained very angry with God for years until one night, when I was in a state of being only half asleep, I had a sort of dream or vision in which I heard God saying, "I am crying for the children even more than you are crying, and I am deeply grieving the suffering of these children with you. What are we

(Continued in next box)

all going to do together?" I began crying. My tears were tears of relief that God was together with me in my grief, that I was joining God in grieving, and that we were grieving together the difficult state of the human journey. I share this to encourage you to always remember that the Divine is grieving with you in your loss and the wounds of our world.

Another spiritual experience that marked me deeply was in my mid-30's. Due to the war in Lebanon, I had already lost my business and the wealth I once had. I had to leave my country, and my marriage also ended. I felt like everything was caving in on me, as if despair was attempting to suffocate me. I came to feel unbelievably raw and alone. I felt completely disconnected from God or any truly supportive presence. Then I realized, as I descended into my grief, that God was right there. The Sacred was truly there with me in the very midst of my sorrow. I had actually never experienced the Divine as close as when I lost everything. It is a memory I will never forget, and it is a memory I always draw on when I begin feeling a sense of disconnection with life. I believe that in the depth of my experience of pain, there is always a loving sacred flame.

~ Chris Saade

I worked with a man who had lost his job and romantic relationship, his parents were both terminally ill, and he was having financial problems. "If this much loss is happening to me at once, where am I being led? Where is life taking me?" he asked. He began to reach out. He reached out to a church community and participated in support groups at our center for grief and hope. He sought out counseling. He looked everywhere he could for meaningful books and studied the lives of people that he respected. He created a sense of community for himself and got involved in giving back.

(Continued in next box)

He helped create an organization for young people that was about mentoring and helping them through his church. He transformed his suffering into an opportunity to create community. But first he had to be willing to reach out. What helps us find the courage to reach out is to know that we have a strength that lives within us which is our refuge. This is spiritual fortitude.

Spiritual fortitude is what has given me hope in those very dark hours when I was afraid, when I was angry, when I was on my knees sobbing. Connecting with the Divine, in my own special and idiosyncratic way, gave me great hope. I was being held, and I was not alone. It has brought me incredible inspiration. It has given me a lot of energy. It has helped me find a sense of meaning where it has been difficult to make sense of things. It is an intuitive logic and a choice—a choice to trust—to trust that this participation in the grief of the world through my own grief is an invitation to learn more about the Divine. This has really helped me in the very long, dark hours of my struggle and suffering.

~ **Mandy McMullen Bird**

Step Six: Service to the World

Act. Through your grief, find your most authentic and pleasurable way of serving freedom, justice, peace, and inclusion. Then take action in the world.

Let love flow through your wounds. When your grief becomes action for love, your spirit grows into its true greatness. Your spirit recovers as you help others recover.

Our losses are a gateway to the depth of our love—love for others and also love for the world. Our grief can seed us with a yearning to give back. Transforming our pain and loss into service for the world is what brings us hope, encouragement, meaning, joy, and deep soul-satisfaction. Our passionate calling to serve freedom, peace, and justice leads us to our true home. This is where our soul longs to reside, and it is our grief that provides an entrance. Our grief is a doorway into that home where so many throughout history have taken their great suffering and used it in service of the soul of the world. It is about service, and it is about generosity. Grief and generous service are bound together. Love-in-action—love as service—is what helps the heart recover!

Unfortunately, too many of us have been indoctrinated with the idea that meaning and service, doing good, or making a difference, all require our sacrifice and suffering. This is a very destructive faulty mindset that so often leads passionate and generous individuals to burnout and despair. What authentically pleasures us is a holy and necessary source of our vital strength and ability to love generously. It is crucial that we refuse to violate the principle of authentic pleasure and trust that there is always a way to love and serve without stress, sacrifice, and suffering. When we stay aligned with our authenticity, including what authentically pleasures us, our capacity to love grows exponentially! When we stand proudly in the truth of what grieves us and what pleasures us, an alchemy of wisdom and strength is unleashed!

This wisdom is needed in the world. It is a wisdom we express through our life-stories. Who better to serve the world than those who are broken-hearted and broken-open by life? The wounded are needed by the world, and we *all* are wounded, so we *all* are needed. By looking within and discovering what will bring meaning to our life, we discover what is missing in the world and how our individual needs can join together in vital partnership with the needs of the world. We all have expertise and gifts that are needed in this world. It is the deep love, called forth by our wounds, which transforms our natural talents and passions from being hidden and withheld to becoming a rich offering of active generosity.

So, while grieving and hurting, act out of love; act out of heart-generosity. An action of human solidarity will further the birth of your own passion. Let such actions spring from the genuine desire of your heart and be aligned with the authenticity of who you are. The transformation from victim to survivor and then to empowered creator takes conscious awareness, recognition, and decisiveness. The grief that breaks our heart open gives us the information we need to serve the world. But we have to make the decision to intentionally act on the longing emerging from our heart. It is our love-in-action which the world awaits. This in turn helps our own personal restoration to life and belonging. Giving generously from the wellspring of what authentically pleasures us brings us a deep-rooted strength and meaning within our lives that we cannot find any other way. When we bestow our authentic generosity on the noble-hearted of the world, our tears are soothed and grief transformed into blessing. If we do not allow our grief to become the doorway to passionate generosity, our grief will fester and remain stale, heavy, and bitter. Passionate and loving action restores the strength and solidity of our heart.

We were created to be an active part of the world's striving toward evolution. This is who we are. This is our genuine humanity. We can refuse to face this reality, but we cannot change it. The Earth created us to be its carriers of blessing and transformation, and it is so important to remember that there is nothing that can replace service. The action of solidarity is what ultimately allows our grief to transform us. Authentic generosity dignifies our humanity. Passionate love-in-action is our soul at its best. So many try to find and create beauty through superficial distractions. Yet it is generous service emerging from our heart's passion where true beauty awaits. It allows us to shed the shell that keeps us imprisoned and to realize that we are one with a force of love so much greater than us. We are part of the world's struggle to achieve a higher level of ethics, and it is our grief that welcomes us home to our most important task.

If we do not hold our loss consciously and act intentionally for service, the loss can lead us to perpetuate cycles of abuse, both of self and others. We can become bitter and cynical and remain trapped in rage and resentment. We can fail to break out of the suffocation of superficiality. It is the respect and honoring of our wounds that can help us practice self-nurturance and act from a place of universal consciousness. If we act in solidarity, we will come to feel very close to others who have known grief on a personal or collective level. For example, when people are struggling and clamoring for justice, we feel more empathic because we know what it means to be deprived.

Our ability to feel empathy with others depends upon how much we are willing to dare being real about the truth of being alive on our planet—the truth of the joy, yet also the pain. It is then that grief becomes love-in-action. Instead of the distanced attitude of judgement always criticizing the imperfections of those who are trying to make a difference, our actions generate empathy with those attempting to help, even if imperfectly, in an imperfect world.

As the heart breaks open, it swells with the waters of compassion and we start to realize that we can give so much love to others; we are no longer limited by a self-image that is personalized and small. We come to realize that our authentic individuality is the twin flame of passionate solidarity—a wide sense of solidarity with the fate of others and our planet. A greater love flows through us when we are in active service to others. So, when we look at people like Sojourner Truth, Harriet Tubman, Eleanor Roosevelt, Mahatma Gandhi, Martin Luther King Jr., and all who worked for democratic freedom, peace, and justice, and if we look at Mother Teresa and the thousands of others who have been part of her battalion of love and activism, we see human beings who have known pain themselves and have allowed that pain to transform them into active agents of peace and justice. Nelson Mandela of South Africa, for example, experienced the tragedy of being imprisoned for decades, separated from his wife, his family, and his friends. But instead of letting this horrendous experience make him sour and blindly vengeful, he allowed it to create in him a higher vision for the liberation of South Africa—one that did not exclude the white population but rather included them in the political process. He came out of prison with a very inclusive, powerful, and compassionate plan to end Apartheid. His broken-open heart enabled him to connect with even more people than he could when he was a younger person in the resistance movement. A different Nelson Mandela was born from that prison experience. His tears were the source of a great passion.

We might not be all called to walk in such auspicious footprints or in such a public way, but in our own space (however small and limited) we can allow our own experience of grief to usher in actions expressing that universal consciousness, that empathic vision, and that passionate compassion. We can become liberated from the chains of the superficial and the meaningless. We can become agents of reconciliation, active for peace and justice through service right where we are—in our larger family systems, corporations, communities, and places of worship. We can speak deeper meaning amongst friends and refuse to just go with the flow of superficial chatter. This action, born out of a wounded and caring heart, is the connection with the higher ethics of love.

There is nothing more fulfilling than to be able to hold the hand (literally or figuratively) of someone who is both noble-hearted and struggling, and to feel at that moment that you have made a difference in their life. There is nothing more fulfilling because, in that act of authentic solidarity, the flow of love streams through us and then cycles back to us in so many ways.

Through the experience of grief, our understanding of what creates human connections and human friendships is transformed. Friendship is no longer simply the idea of sharing the same interests or sharing the same usual stories. Instead of such a superficial view of friendship, we begin, through our own vulnerability, to connect with our common human vulnerability. Friendship becomes the sharing of open hearts solidified by the appreciation of each other's character. At its highest level, it is enriched through the generous giving and receiving of love, by working together for social and ecological transformation, and by encouraging each other's sense of service and passion. Friendship becomes a sharing of souls—real and genuine—and a mutual respect for each person's genuine struggles, tears, hopes, breakdowns, and breakthroughs. Authenticity becomes the precious jewel instead of social posturing and games. We cultivate our wound to become the *womb* for the best in us, and the best of our vision, to emerge and grow. We become people of action striving to build the world of our dreams. Cynicism and apathy are replaced by imperfect action, yet action that is most worthy! May we keep in mind that action emerging from a loving heart may not always achieve the results we hoped for, but it will definitely empower, enrich, and soothe our own wounds and be a gift to others and the world. Such action will carve out more space for freedom and audacity in the sanctuary of our soul. We create and are created by the actions of our love. We are made to become the best version of ourselves through these daring actions of love and solidarity.

A tool to help you manifest your grief into acts of generosity is to read stories and talk to others who have gone through similar circumstances. Reading memoirs, autobiographies, and biographies of individuals who have had similar struggles with grief, and through their own challenges offer insight and inspiration. Finding organizations supportive of those who are enduring the same loss or struggle can also be very helpful. Making these connections is invaluable because it helps us relate to the larger community around us, helps us find inspiration, and shows us areas where service has made a difference and where our service is needed. Many times when we have experienced a deep loss, the very place that we are called to serve is the same area where we experienced our own loss. Service often materializes through honoring a lost loved one. Act in the name of and in honor of your grief.

"How do we make sure that the pain and suffering of our grief really ends up blessing us?" The answer to this question is: Authentic generosity. Honoring and listening to our grief brings our passion to light, and our passion reveals what is authentically calling us. Following our calling becomes the blessing. Implementing our calling is essential for us to feel hope and empowerment through our difficult days. It is our calling that keeps us going. Our calling carries an energy in itself that infuses us with vitality and a rich sense of soulful reward. Following our calling matures our spirit, brings forth more of our humanity, and deepens our authenticity.

One woman we met through our non-profit organization lost her husband suddenly and unexpectedly. She was left the single mother of two daughters. Her husband's great passion had been entrepreneurship, so she decided to start a foundation that teaches urban youth and intercity children entrepreneurial skills. She developed an entire mentoring program. Out of her husband's sudden and unexpected death, she asked herself, "How can I honor this man that I love, and how can I give back to the world in honor of his memory and his passion?" Her calling helped her integrate her grief and brought her inspiration and empowerment.

At the *Institute for Life-Leadership and Coaching* where we both hold consulting positions, we repeatedly witness how acts of passion arise from heart-tears. One of our colleagues, a school social worker, musician, poet, and dear friend, used his passion (born out of his grief of losing his mother at a young age as well as his profound sadness for impoverished children) to create a powerful vision of authenticity and solidarity. He created several musical CDs inspiring participants at the *Institute* as well as the children in his school. He adjusted the leadership training to fit the younger kids. Eventually he organized an excellent leadership training on authenticity and solidarity and is making it available for disenfranchised students.

What was born from his conscious grieving is most admirable and an invaluable gift to the community and students! This is what this step is about—mining your grief for greater wisdom and clarity on your path of service. Your sacred grief is inviting you to follow its lead into action.

The next tool is the exploration of avenues of service. Explore both through your imagination and the concrete reality of your circumstances. Through your imagination, try to see the ways of serving that are most exciting to you as well as the most authentic. Service arises from your wounds, but *how* you serve must bring you some level of joy and lots of fulfillment. The form your service takes also needs to fit your own unique authenticity. You can never serve and make a lasting difference out of a sense of guilt or forced obligation. Your serving must be an expression of your own individual authenticity, unique gifts, and passions. Sometimes service is an avocation. Sometimes it is a vocation you wish to pursue. Other times it might be a partial expression within what you already do. For example, an artist might focus a portion of her paintings on the theme of social solidarity. A potter could dedicate some of his work to raise funds for a school for the blind. My [Chris Saade's] daughter, who is an actress and teacher, often participates in theatre projects dedicated to empowering the elderly, homeless, and children with special needs. A lawyer can offer a good amount of his time defending underprivileged immigrants.

On the level of concrete exploration, make a list of organizations where you could volunteer that seem authentically interesting to you. Then go and spend some time at your favorites. Experiment with different places where you can serve and see how they feel to you; find out what fits your spirit and your nature.

There is a common misconception expressed by the frequently asked question: "How can I help others when I am so broken and grief-stricken?" It is precisely then that you can do your best work. It is through the tears that open our heart that we can best hear others in their pain. It is through our vulnerability that we can offer our strength in support of others during very vulnerable times. The best public speakers are not those who put on a positive face, but those who speak to us through their "realness."' Remember a new type of human being is emerging in our world—one that is very strong through their vulnerability and very loving through their wounds. Our newly emerging humanity knows the power of authenticity—authenticity of self and heart!

Another story to illustrate this point is about Father Pierre's work in France. Pierre was a Catholic priest who was part of the Resistance during WWII and founded the Emmaus movement in 1949 with the intention of helping homeless people and refugees. He was renowned and respected internationally for his political activism and his charitable organization. During a ferociously cold winter in France in 1954, when homeless people were dying in the streets, he organized what would become known as "an uprising of kindness." Through a radio program, he called on all French people to radically flood the distribution centers of charities with clothes and food. The response was most amazing and unseen before! The streets of Paris were overtaken by donors. He was also politically gifted and met with leaders around the world, including President Eisenhower, but he never strayed from his immediate connection to those in need. What was striking about his message is that he would go to the neediest of people and say, "Come and help me help others." He would invite the homeless to work on building homes for others in need, because, he said, it is when we are broken that we can give the most. He knew how offering love feeds us. We engage in service because it helps others, while just as importantly, it builds our own strength, soothes our wounds, and nurtures our heart.

While preparing yourself to express your love-in-action, you can also think about or pray eagerly for those who are suffering from the same loss from which you are suffering, thus entering into caring communion with them and expanding your sense of being part of the wounded human race. When you are in pain, think of or pray for others. This sense of care connects our spirits in more ways than we can understand.

Channel the grief of your heart and transmute it into a passionate voice for love, reconciliation, justice, peace, and solidarity. Let your voice speak in as many ways as possible. For example, in your place of worship you could ask to speak about your experience and how it is helping you become a person of greater solidarity and compassion. You can honor the grief of others and thus help people overcome the shame they have about their own grief. Unfortunately, in many religious or spiritual communities, there is a spoken or subtle injunction to always be "positive," thus blocking our powerful and paradoxical authenticity. Another way of countering this destructive message is through writing; you can write letters to the editor, online blogs, poetry, or prose. Tom Anthony, the current Director of the *Institute for Life-Leadership and Coaching*, has known a great deal of grief in his life—including serious challenges with his health. He chose to passionately and generously express his pain through his poetry. He wrote through his poems about his own journey of grief as well as that of others. His poetry became a profound gift for those going through similar experiences as well as to the community at large. His writing became a river of transformation—for himself and for so many others.

It touches us in the depth of our soul to receive words of support from people who deeply care for us or who are witnessing what is happening to us on our journey. In our modern culture, social media, texting, messaging, and emails are all ways you can reach out, support others, and be a powerful voice for your vision of love and eco-social solidarity. There is also always the traditional pen-and-ink writing of letters. The point is to take the words of your own heart and put them into action. So when you are thinking, "What is it that I need right now?" look around at those you love and those you have met in the community and give them words and actions of honoring and encouragement. It is a powerful way to begin serving.

Yet another thing you can do is to become a support to others who are doing humanitarian or meaningful hands-on work. Let them know you are aware of their efforts and offer appreciation for their dedication. We need to remember that everyone who is out there trying to make a difference needs a lot of support. Remember that we are all connected. We are all one in many ways, and as much as you bless others, you are blessed. As much as you support others, you are supported. As much as you honor others, you are honored. Leaders need support. Pioneers need support. Active support is an act of generosity and heart-activism!

Stories of grief translating into love-in-action unfold everywhere, every day. One leader in our community took the grief she experienced from racial prejudice and created a series of greeting cards that celebrate diversity in all manner of ways—racial, gender, sexual, and cultural—as a way of expressing empathy and solidarity with those who experience exclusion. She allowed that voice arising in her to a be gift to the community. On a national level we can see many heartbroken and brave parents—individuals who have tragically lost their children to the insanity of gun violence—take a strong stand for gun control and find in their grief the courage to challenge the big money entities invested in the gun trade. We also are witnessing the amazing increase in participation of young students grieving their friends in school massacres. They are speaking out and finding the strength and stamina, arising from their tears, to act and march peacefully, yet resolutely and powerfully, to Washington D.C.

A clearer vision of meaningful action can come through us when we are in a place of grief. Let this vision become a passionate voice in you. Let it become action. Remember that times of great grief are sacred and bring creative power that belongs to the community and is needed by the community. In many ancient beliefs, the grief of a person did not belong to them alone, it belonged to the tribe because they understood that great revelations come through deep grief and that these revelations need to be shared for the benefit of all. This tradition is a reminder to the individual that these great and challenging experiences do not belong solely to them. Your grief is experienced by you, but it belongs to and connects you with the world. It belongs to the communities in which you participate.

One of the facilitators and leaders at the *Institute of Life-Leadership and Coaching* lost her husband when she was six months pregnant. It marked her life with grief and the deepest of wounds. Ultimately, she consecrated her life to do her own inner work and to mine the gifts of that grief, eventually becoming a powerful leadership trainer and a teacher. In addition to her leadership and teaching, she made it a point to powerfully support those in her community doing good work in the world. What we learn through the mystery and power of love, and through allowing love to flow through our heart toward others—even in the moments of our greatest need—is that it all comes back to us because we are part of the same circle of life. Service and giving back to others through our grief and pain supports our life in unimaginable ways. As we work at healing the world, we enrich our own spirit. As we let our tears become an even greater passion of love, we come to know life at a much deeper level—life at its essence!

It is self-empowering to be of service, however, it is also important to remember that serving the causes of social justice, peace, ecological sustainability, and so forth is an honor and privilege. It is a great privilege to participate in the unfolding of love in the world!

I have taught and trained psychotherapists and healing professionals for almost 20 years, and one crucial thing I share with them is that some of the best work they do is when they are in touch with their own grief and their own wounds. I suggest they do not put their sadness away in order to be there for their clients. Therapists help the most when they are in relationship with their own grief. They are most there for others when they are intentionally present through whatever feeling-state they are experiencing. Their grief can become a source of their passionate actions toward helping others. We help through our grief and because of our grief, not in spite of it!

How beautiful it is when a person who is experiencing the loss of a relationship empathizes with other people who are experiencing a similar loss of a relationship—or when somebody who is struggling with illness reaches out to others struggling with an illness. I have been

(Continued in next box)

very challenged by a severe chronic migraine, and one thing that has really helped me when I was (or am) struggling the most is to spend time thinking and praying for others who are also struggling with chronic illnesses. I had a lot of support for my health challenge, and I know there are many others who do not have such support. Bringing others into my consciousness helped greatly. It took me out of personalization and isolation and put me in a spiritual communion with others who suffer and in solidarity and kinship with other souls. I felt their courage strengthening mine and their hopes feeding mine. The awareness of my own shakiness and the pain of others has fueled my writing all through my illness. I wanted my writing to be a contribution, an action born out of my own life grief and hope and sustained by the will of my wounded body.

~ Chris Saade

In August of 2017 my beloved friend Kristi died from stage four breast cancer. It was absolutely heartbreaking for me to lose my precious friend and soul sister so young, too soon. The day before she died, I called a small non-profit named Turning Point whose mission is to help women who have been domestically abused make a new start in life. I asked them if they would partner with me and Kristi's other dear friends to create a fundraiser in Kristi's honor. I knew I had to put into practice what I have been teaching and training others to do all these years. I knew deep down in my bones that doing a fundraiser for this non-profit in her honor would help me hold the pain and help to bring some meaning to losing my friend way before she was ready to die. It was an amazing experience! In March of 2018, the month that Kristi would have turned 55, we raised thousands of dollars at a celebratory fundraiser. Accessing Kristi's beautiful life as inspiration and using my grief as fuel to give back to this most worthy organization

(Continued in next box)

brought so much encouragement to me and her dear friends and family. It truly is amazing what can be created from our deep grief.

~ **Mandy McMullen Bird**

Step Seven: Celebrate

Celebrate your WHOLE life—the entirety of your authentic journey rich in losses and blessings, defeats and successes.

Celebrate your whole life and the life of your loved ones, with its pain and joys. Celebrate that most genuine and worthy canvas of your humanity!

In Japan, many broken objects are repaired with gold. The flaw is seen as part of the object's total beauty, even as an addition to its beauty. The whole is valued rather than just the unbroken part!

The final step in heart-centered grieving is to *celebrate* our passage through grief as well as celebrate our, so normal and so human, wounded (and creative) life-journey. This final step is an advanced one in the grief process; it finds its place only after honoring the tears that opened our heart. Celebration is not usually something to explore at the beginning of the grief journey; it comes with time and as the calling of the heart emerges. Entering, exploring, and transmuting our grief is a journey of an initiation that unfurls more of our authenticity and leads us to our calling in the world (or to a deeper understanding of our calling). We are also invited into the nature of paradox—the relationship between grief and joy and how these support each other. Grief is profoundly individual; each one of us grieves very differently, however we can always choose to mine our grief as a soul deepening experience.

To be clear, what we are celebrating here is neither the loss nor the pain as such. We are celebrating the whole journey of life and the gifts that come from a life fully and courageously lived—because life includes loss, grief, defeats, successes, and breakdowns, as well as significant breakthroughs. We celebrate the fullness of life, the realization that life is an intricate web of connected events and experiences—including those which are *very painful.* There is laughter and smiles of deep contentment. There are also tears. There will continue to be moments of tremendous excitement and moments of deep sorrow. Knowing this, we come to a place in our life where we say a heroic "Yes!" to life. We come to know how to profoundly honor our tears and our joy as part of the epic journey of the spirit. We revere our authenticity, our individuality, and our authentic unique story. Celebration can only happen when we look at and feel our loss through our heart. Otherwise our loss can make us bitter and cynical, and we can miss mining our grief's great gifts toward growth and evolution. No matter if your loss is a job, a person, a relationship, or health-related, if you courageously allow it to open your heart, you are heroic.

It is so essential to remember, in the context of our grief, that celebration is about pride in our brave life choices and in the force of life within us. It is also a prayer of the heart. We celebrate the strength, generosity, and capacity to love that we have developed. We give thanks for what is deeply beautiful in this life, for the Earth, and for our paradoxical journey on this planet. This includes life *and* death; it includes the warmth of spring and the chill of winter. It is the whole process. Celebration becomes an offering of a beautiful and authentic song of the heart through our smiles and our tears. There is so much phony "looking good" spirituality these days. It is like an epidemic of false smiles and false statements implying, "I am always doing great." Our spirits are hungry for a return to authenticity—a return to people who will share themselves in their full humanity, their incredible strength as well as their vulnerability. Such authenticity is the requirement for true and lasting love, be it in romance, friendship, or in our community. There is no love without celebrating our authenticity, and there is no authenticity without claiming our tears with grace and honoring and being proud of our human journey through deep wounds and moments of great joy. It is about celebrating the life force within our tears, our disappointments, as well as within our deepest joys and pleasures.

So how exactly do we celebrate when our heart is filled with grief? It is a radical step and it is extremely important not to push ourselves before we are ready. It is not about leaving sorrow behind. It is also not about seeking out a pretend happiness. It is about being internally ready to know your grief in its full dignity. Life is incomplete without celebration. It is essential to keep in mind that you are not betraying yourself or your loss when you feel moved internally to challenge yourself and say, "I want to hold the fullness of my journey, grief and joy. I want to celebrate my authentic spirit and the mystery of life as well!"

Celebration is not a denial of grief! On the contrary it is an affirmation of life and the relationship we have with the fullness of our humanity. Sometimes it is difficult to wrap our mind around how completely legitimate it is to celebrate after we have had a difficult time and suffered severe loss. Yet the celebration of our journey through our tears destroys shame and upholds the great dignity of a noble human life. It is also a great modeling to our children that they can deal with their challenges, defeats, and losses without giving up on or diminishing the beauty of their life. We can show them that they can celebrate who they are and their unique walk through life with all of the often-painful difficulties of growing up. It is only when we befriend the human reality of grief and make it the companion of joy in our heart that we can come to know the breadth and depth of the celebration of life and love.

In our work with clients, after people move through the first six steps it becomes a natural inclination to get to a point of self-observation and say, "Look how far I have come. Look how much my spirit has grown. Look how much I have expanded my heart and vision." This is all worth celebrating.

This step of celebration is about claiming the right to your entire life. No part of it needs to be shut out or closed off. As you gently integrate your grief, you can begin to make small strides toward celebrating your life and journey. Sometimes you have to pursue it gradually. It is a retraining of our brain to say: "My grief is part of the rich colors in my life's canvas. It is an intrinsic part of my humanity. I will honor my grief, not belittle it, and never stop upholding and celebrating the dignity of my journey! I will also honor the grief of others and support and join them in speaking its voice!"

This approach is also crucial to how we learn to hold the collective grief in our country and our world: We are called to honor it, to respect it, to give it a voice, and to celebrate our collective strides forward without feeling that to do so, we have to cover up and diminish the grief. We can celebrate our countries and democracies with their mistakes and breakdowns while fully acknowledging and making valid the grief pertaining to these failures. It is very important today in our defense of democracy to celebrate its ideals and institutions with all their grievous imperfection.

As we affirm the dignity and richness of our own grief, it helps a great deal to find ways to celebrate others—family members, friends, members of our community—for the sensitivity, dignity, and courage of their spirit throughout their grief and struggle.

All of your losses and all of your suffering can be mined for profound, life-giving, and liberating treasure. You have the power to extract the wisdom and blessing from the cauldron of your pain. The scars of your wounds, through your lionhearted dedication, are woven into the fabric of who you are, what you are about, where you are being called, and how you are connected to everyone in the world. This is our beautiful, paradoxical human story, and our creative responses to it are undoubtedly something to celebrate with immense pride. Do not let one ounce of your story go by without taking the time to say, "This matters, and I matter," and marking it with celebration.

One practical tool to help along this step of celebration in the face of our deepest sorrows is to visit places of natural beauty and remember how, in the fall or winter, nature grieves and has its own losses. The trees lose their leaves, many things die, but the loss and the death prepare for new birth and the emergence of spring. Winter, in all its barrenness, is pregnant with vibrant, resplendent colors hidden within its grieving scenery. It is all a part of the paradoxical reality of our existence, and all of the seasons are to be celebrated in their richness. Take time to see this beauty; it reflects your own human beauty. You are as beautiful when you are grieving as a priceless painting of fall or winter or as nature itself. Take the time to reflect upon the beauty of your ability to harbor deep sorrow as well as to be the womb of many springs.

A very important concern that needs to be addressed now is: "Will celebration be disrespectful of my losses or the loved ones I have lost in my life?" The answer is absolutely, "No." To the contrary, celebration is a way of honoring your losses and the memory of those you love. Celebration honors what your loved ones have contributed to you, and it also honors the sacredness of the relationship—the time and the experiences that you had together, whatever the losses. Celebration affirms that in any situation there is a gem of beauty and meaning that can never be lost. Take, for example, a relationship where there was genuine love, yet the relationship ended. It might have ended in a very sad and difficult way, yet without denying the pain, you can find gems of beauty. Celebration affirms these gems. Celebration can affirm the beauty of the other's spirit or your own investment of love. Celebration affirms that those who are lost are still alive in you in some way. Remember, the people you have lost in your life do not want you to give up on life. They want you to remember them with the tears of grief *and* with the joy and celebration for everything that was shared.

We are asked to remember that life was present not only before and after, but during and within the losses themselves, and that passion is born from our tears. In the coaching circles we have led, we have witnessed some couples choosing to end their relationship. In the

One time, I watched a woman perform as a professional dancer. She had experienced great loss in her life. Her son had just been diagnosed with a very difficult illness and she was scheduled to perform that evening. She chose not to cancel the performance. She declared to the audience her vulnerable situation. She started dancing, then danced with tears flowing down her face. Grief and tears overwhelmed her, and she kept on dancing and dancing passionately. At one point in the dance she raised her hands in celebration with tears still shining like jewels on her cheeks. The audience then stood up and exploded in loud acclamations. Women and men started crying. We all felt that amazing and sacred moment. The critics later could not hold back their praise. This is heart-centered grief: celebrating with our tears and celebrating the beauty of the tears themselves. It is the totality of our deeply authentic experience of life that matters, the totality of our valiant journey which deserves the full dignity and honor of celebration. As we claim our humanity, we transcend both superficial vanity and spiritual hypocrisy. We become stout, strong, wise, and sensitive in our human heart. We become people who do not have to hide their real life in secrecy. We become transparent to ourselves and others. We generously offer our story and our struggles. Shame is overcome.

~ Chris Saade

sacred space of an authentic community, they were able, even with their grief and anger, to celebrate the genuine love they each had for the other and to celebrate all that was so beautiful and alive between them. Some have even been able to celebrate the fact that their ex-partner found a new partner. It was truly astounding to witness the power and dignity the act of intentional celebration can bring.

The celebration of our full journey is not a negation of the wound; it is a most life-giving container for the wound. Even our defeats must ultimately be celebrated—defeats in our work, relationships, or in our eco-political involvement. Defeats, when claimed honestly and intentionally, are the steps on the ladder for greater achievement and greater love. When we learn to celebrate our defeats and teach our children to do so, we (and our young ones) become much bolder in our love and our actions toward our vision. Through celebration, we impassion our struggle (its good days and hard days), free our inevitable creative defeats from shame, and deeply dignify our lives.

Grief can be very deep. We need to descend into that grief, feel it, and create a space for it in the landscape of our authenticity. We need to know that life always surrounds us, the Source of life surrounds us, and beauty still surrounds us. Ultimately, what we are asked to do is deepen the full intensity of our feelings while unleashing the fullness of our passion in service of others and in celebration of our journey forward. Nothing is to be held back—not our grief, not our suffering, and certainly not our appreciation for the beauty of love and our passion to make a difference. Let the fullness of existence be alive within you. What weakens you is holding back your genuine heart feelings; when you hold back the feeling of sadness, you start to hold back the feelings of joy and love, of passion and the ability to celebrate. As you learn to live with the fullness of your authenticity, your heart evolves immensely in its ability to love and serve passionately.

There is no place to hide. It is about befriending all of your life. This includes making space for the fullness of your grief—the losses, defeats, and your angst and outrage at oppression and abuse—while keeping your heart completely open and deeply at peace with its own story. Remember it is the refusal to befriend your grief that stops you from fully unearthing your precious and unique authenticity! When you are ready to welcome all of your feelings and states of being, you will experience the fullness of your humanity and be on your way to unabashedly celebrating it.

Celebrating your life and the life of others, no matter what has happened, is an incredible blessing. It is a huge statement of love for your own spirit and the spirit of others. It is an affirmation of how valuable every noble journey of soul, self, and heart is to the Universe.

It is important that you let go of the judgments and biases that say your life is only worth celebrating under certain conditions. The essence of who you are—your worthiness, the sacredness within your life, and the sacredness within your grief—deserves full celebration, unconditionally.

Another thing to celebrate wholeheartedly is a deeper connection with the Divine and/or with the deepest essence of your self. It is often during times of great grief and suffering, when you are most broken-hearted and unable to ask for support, that you can experience the Divine and your own being in such a transparent and intimate way. This is the time when you can breathe in gratitude for unwavering divine love. Tolstoy, the 19th century Russian writer and philosopher said, "Love life, for to love life despite all its tragedies is to love God."

You can also celebrate how you, through your woundedness, are choosing to pour out even greater and more potent love. Through your flowing tears, if you do not stifle them, your ability to love and be passionate has significantly grown—and love is the greatest jewel of your existence.

A tool which can be very helpful here is calling friends you trust and inviting them to share a dinner with you dedicated to the celebration of your journey through grief and struggle. Rather than hide it, speak it out with pride. This is an incredible mentoring for your children and for your loved ones. In our culture, we need to start celebrating not only successes, not only the new relationship or birth of a child, but also our personal and collective wounds, losses and, defeats on the way forward. Start with small steps, and then, gradually, expand the celebration.

We receive deep rewards through exploring the important questions that we have considered in this chapter: "How can I celebrate when my heart is filled with grief? Will celebration dishonor my losses or my loved ones? What do I celebrate when my heart is broken?" As you continue to explore the answers, you will truly be taken to the edge of your spiritual growth.

The very best in us is fashioned and sculpted by our challenges and our difficulties. In our modern culture, sadly we do not respect the challenges, the difficulties, or the wounds we suffer. Yet we come to life to be sculpted. Through it all, we can choose to determinedly unleash our highest authentic self—we can become wiser, stronger, more passionately loving, and most caring for justice and solidarity. It is this heroic journey that we must fully claim, honor, and celebrate.

It is important to acknowledge the parts in each of us that resist this step of celebration. When we are broken-hearted and grieving, it is not easy to start thinking about celebration. It doesn't even compute at times. There are parts in us that resist *because celebration is an evolutionary step*. The unconditional "Yes!" is an extremely big deal. It matters for the whole consciousness of humanity that we learn to hold celebration while grieving and resist pushing either aside. To intentionally choose great meaning in our life, regardless of what has happened or is happening, takes courage and deserves great respect.

We can adamantly resist celebrating when we are wounded and lost, but there is a deeper place in our heart that knows the wisdom of embracing the fullness of our life in all its complexity. It is from this depth of our heart that we assume the power and the dignity of our full humanity, a grounded affirmation that becomes the blessing in our own life as well as in the lives of our loved ones and community.

Some of the most personally meaningful workshops and retreats I have taught are those I have had the privilege of facilitating with widows—young widows in particular—who have suffered the tragic loss of their beloved. As intense as it is, and as frightening at times, sitting with that much pain with other human beings always brings the light of the Divine right there to that spot.

There is a closeness between us as we gather together and move through the steps of heart-centered grief and the power of celebration. There is such a closeness between us all as we recognize how precious and sacred life is in those moments as we experience the Divine together.

We connect through our shattered states and share how difficult it is to even recognize ourselves. Then we celebrate the beauty of our lives and how we are claiming more of our full authentic selves from the ashes of our pain. We celebrate that we would not be able to be who we are today, and who we are becoming, without the deep courage and support to mine our heartbreaking personal experiences.

~ Mandy McMullen Bird

When I was serving in the peace movement, I knew of a person who was imprisoned just because he belonged to a different faith. He struggled with claustrophobia. He was in prison for about nine months. When he was released, he shared that in the beginning of his imprisonment he did not know how he would survive confinement. This was a person who loved life so much! Then he said he started to look around in his cell to see what could be appreciated or celebrated. He started with the wall and saw it was old and made of brick, and there were cracks in it. He saw beauty in that old wall that was his "home" in prison. He started celebrating the beauty of the wall itself, its

(Continued in next box)

architecture, and imagining how time had affected that wall. Then he found other things that he could appreciate. He spent time remembering beautiful past moments with his family and also imagining future possibilities of love and tender intimacy. By celebrating all that he could, he found the strength to feel and hold his grief, and to stay alive. What he celebrated did not turn his experience into a "positive" one. It just made it real (and so powerfully authentic), with both sides of all his humanity: beauty and grief, grief and beauty! This is what we must remember. The more we celebrate, the more we are able to descend safely into our grief and thus to find and retrieve the sacred and creative treasures of our grief.

~ **Chris Saade**

Epilogue

The journey through heart-centered grief requires your attention to all seven steps. Step One: Affirm Your Grief; Step Two: Open Your Heart; Step Three: Initiation; Step Four: Paradox; Step Five: Spiritual Fortitude; Step Six: Service; Step Seven: Celebration of Life. Experiencing your grief through a courageous and open heart allows you to know the fullness of your human feelings without falling prey to a sense of victimization or hidden rage. You will become more intimate with strength, love, generous passion, and a deeper sense of calling.

It takes time to integrate these ideas. They are very different from what we have been culturally, and often spiritually, taught about how to handle our grief journey. In fact, we are told too many times to avoid our grief and not to engage it or befriend it. Heart-centered grief and hope take time, patience, gentleness toward your wounds, and a sturdy commitment to yourself. It takes rejecting shame and being very respectful of your humanity. It also takes becoming your own best ally—moving through your grief journey with dignity—as you claim the beauty of your life and the nobility of *all* of your human story.

Remember that your heart and your spirit are very tender and vulnerable when you are going through the difficulty of grief and loss. Life has treasures of beauty, but life is also very hard and challenging. So be the best friend you can be to your authentic self. Be at peace with the timing of your process. Above all, be genuine and act with love and for a vision of love. The grief journey is part of the story of both individuals and cultures. Trust your own knowing, the wisdom, the passion, and the calling emerging from your tears.

Today, on a collective level, we are so much in need of claiming our grief about poverty, all kinds of ugly prejudices, serious ecological pollution, the neglect of millions of children, the serious threat to our democracies, religious violence, terrorism, and other crucial issues. Without feeling the grief of our collective wounds, we will not passionately act or sustain our actions with strength and peaceful resolve. We direly need to claim this grief, honor its dignity, and speak its wisdom and calling. Despair will paralyze and imprison us in a helpless victim mentality. But a conscious and intentional grief will awaken very powerful and creative, passionate and peaceful forces in us!

The most valuable thing in life by far, is the heart. We are most blessed to encounter the heart in others, the heart in ourselves, the heart in the world, and the heart of the Divine. This entire journey is to support you in opening your heart, expanding it to its furthest horizons, and unleashing its passion to love, to build tender partnerships, and to serve. This very human journey of befriending your grief will help you connect with the calling of your heart and contribute to peace, freedom, authenticity, justice, social solidarity, inclusion, ecological responsibility, and the transformation of consciousness.

Without feeling our wounds and integrating our grief as part of our humanity, we numb out and stunt our intelligence. We have to reassert that we become fully human when we befriend our grief and know the grief of the world. Without integrating our grief and our core wounds (along with our joys and our hopes) as part of the unique and beautiful canvas of who we are, we cannot fully embody our caring humanity and build deeply loving relationships. We cannot grow our heart—which is the most important part of our evolution. It is the open heart which, with a developed and informed mind, can lead us forward into a sturdy democracy and sustainable ecology. The superficiality of the fake social life with its endless games and the destructive practice of "positive" thinking (childish denial) will lead our culture to its demise. Following that path, we will lose our democracy and destroy our environment. For it is only those who know grief and can bear it well who will be able to take on the difficult tasks needed for a global vision of love. Only our real and authentic humanity—with its deeply felt grief and hopes, with its openness of heart and profundity of mind—will allow us to respond to the challenges threatening us.

We cannot offer love or empathy, nor experience the magic of romance and the sweetness of physical intimacy, if we repress our deep feelings. When grief is acknowledged and honored, it becomes a noble and productive part of us both individually and collectively. If covered up, it leads to destructive and lethal unconscious trends. As we have explored throughout this book, on the one hand, the suppression of grief on a personal or cultural level will undoubtedly lead to depression, rage, and physical ailments, and on a political level, to a backlash of fascistic rage. On the other hand, when grief is acknowledged and the painful struggle of marginalized groups is dignified and honored, healing and reconciliation have a serious chance to occur.

Our feelings will only have a chance to mature if we bring them to consciousness and learn to express them with respect and grace. We are all wounded. The noblest of hearts are wounded. We are wounded lovers, wounded friends, wounded activists, wounded healers, wounded artists, and wounded leaders. However, those who are conscious of their wounds, who respect them and let them become the source of greater love and a larger passionate vision, these are the women and men who can lead us into a sustainable and non-violent future—a future where care is central and the forces of oppression are put on their heels. We cannot lie about our wounded existential condition as human beings. The truth must be named in order to shine, transform, and bless us.

As you go through the grieving process with an open heart, you discover more of what you are here on Earth to do. You will come to embody your priceless humanity. You will know more intimately your destiny and the meaning of your life. As you remain tender with your own wounds, you will become tender with the wounds of your love partner, your children, and the world. By being fiercely true to yourself in your authenticity, you will perceive more of your calling, you will love from your heart, support others in their authentic journey, and receive love back. You will feel sustained by love. Love and love-in-action will become the primary reality of your life, and your humanity will unfold with an ever-greater presence of that force of love.

Chris Saade is an author, a psychological and philosophical teacher, a life coach, and a trainer of professionals. He was previously an entrepreneur, a director of nonprofits, and a peace activist. After many years serving as a psychotherapist in private practice, Saade spent two decades training therapists, coaches, and the general public in two of his models: ***Integra: 6 Keys for Heart-Centered Living***, and ***The Quest for Individual Authenticity and Global Solidarity.***

To date, Saade has led nearly 250 multi-day cutting-edge workshops for professionals and the general public. He currently writes and offers life-coaching and teaching.

Saade has a BA in economics, a master's degree in human development and learning with a focus in counseling, and an additional five years of graduate studies in theology, economics, and history.

Born in Beirut, Lebanon, he was involved in peace and humanitarian work for 14 years before and during the Lebanese war. The difficulty of those times taught Saade to approach great challenges from the heart and through service. This led him to develop a great respect for freedom, authenticity, diversity, peace, and a passion for justice and solidarity, especially for children.

Saade's legacy book ***Rebellion of the Heart*** with artist Katie Cassette was published in 2020. His other titles include: ***Second Wave Spirituality:*** *Passion for Peace, Passion for Justice;* and ***Prayers for Peace and Justice;*** as well as ***Prayers from the Heart***. He co-authored ***Evolutionary Love Relationships:*** *Passion, Authenticity, and Activism* with Andrew Harvey in 2017. The Saade-Harvey team has also co-created two recordings: ***Sacred Activism and the Epic Spirituality of Love***, available on CD, and ***An Evolutionary Vision of Relationships*** available as CD or digital download. An additional artbook focusing on love relationships created in collaboration with the photographic artist, Ginger Wagoner, is scheduled for release later this year.

Saade is a father of a very beloved daughter and grandfather to two wonderful boys. He resides in San Diego.

Mandy McMullen Bird is a licensed therapist in private practice for 30 years. She devotes herself to counseling individuals, couples, and families struggling with the effects of depression, anxiety, grief, sexual abuse, and trauma. She specializes in guiding and supporting her clients in discovering their own authentic voice and is an accredited Grief Expert.

Emphasizing education in cutting-edge psychological tools and techniques for dialoguing, Mandy excels in helping her clients grow emotionally and offers profound assistance to those in crisis. She has led numerous groups, workshops, and retreats around themes such as self-esteem, grief and loss, personal empowerment, communication and intimacy, and career and life visions.

For two years, Mandy was regularly featured on Matt & Ramona's nation-wide syndicated radio show as "Counselor Mandy." Listeners called in to ask for her opinion, guidance, encouragement, and compassion on a wide variety of issues. Inspired by the number of listeners she was able to reach, she began the radio show "Finding Hope" on eWN Radio Network hosting notable guests who openly shared their passionate journeys of loss, joy, soul-growth, and leadership. This morphed into the "Finding Hope" podcast which can be found on all major listening platforms.

Since childhood, Mandy has been called to support, witness, and acknowledge those in deep pain. She considers her work sacred. An outgrowth of this calling was to co-found *The Respite, A Women's Resource for Loss & Hope*, a non-profit which served individuals in her community for several years.

Mandy Bird is a teacher, guide, and companion on the road of grief, healing, and discovering one's Authentic Nature to be given in Service of the World. She lives near Charlotte, NC with her husband Glenn, where they are enjoying the adventure of a blended family with 3 daughters: Emily, Maddy, and Tess, along with their dog Ginny.

As a companion to this book, we invite you to listen to **Season 4** of the **Finding Hope Podcast**, hosted by Mandy Bird and including episodes with Chris Saade as one of the featured guests. Here you will find eight, 30-minute episodes that focus on the content of this book, bringing it to life with engaging conversations and stories from people who have used the 7-Steps as a guide in their grief journey. You can find the podcast at: anchor.fm/findinghope and on all major podcast channels including Apple Podcasts and Spotify.

Made in the USA
Columbia, SC
16 November 2022

71425827R00122